Imaginative Spasms:

The Postmodern Poems of

Scott Alderson

Imaginative Spasms

Library and Archives Canada Cataloguing in Publication

Alderson, Scott, 1964-

Imaginative spasms / Scott Alderson.

ISBN Paperback: 978-0-9682712-8-5

Kindle: 978-0-9682712-9-2

1. Postmodern poetry

2. Poetry

Printed and bound in Canada.

Dedication

This work is dedicated to my hero, my brother Kevin. Through the dark and the light his spirit shines.

Reflection

Pray for a cure for multiple sclerosis.

Table of Contents

2017

When the dream ended
woke with wheelchair
welcoming my swollen frame
pounds prior and years past
reality is immobility
looking to a cloudy sky to ask,
"What happened, where did I go wrong?"

When the day subsided
non-nourishing nightsweats
soaked sheets of my non-custom bed
sought gratitude and willingness
to replace negative thoughts inside my head
imaginative spasms followed.

Three Small White Mice Travelling at the Speed of Light

Copyright 1994

Authors Note – This work is dedicated to my wife Stephanie and my son Danann for their continual love and support.

Three Small White Mice, Travelling at the Speed of Light

Someone knocked at my door yesterday,
while my clock radio uttered sounds
they told me it was Christmas
but no one was around.

I asked them in for coffee
they said they wanted tea
I ask what they were after,
they said they had come for me.

Asking to be taken
I was amazed to find
that I could not wake up
from this bizarre dream of mine.

Led into our galaxy
on this our Christmas Day
I was pulled by some force
forced to obey.

Led into a gloomy star
looking mean not nice
I was approached
by three small mice.

Three Small White Mice Travelling at the Speed of Light

Beckoning me to follow them
destroying all my might,
these small mice
travelled at the speed of light.

We raced around the Universe
for what seemed to me a year,
suddenly I was back in my bed
beside me was a beer.

Destroying my clock radio
a nuisance as such,
realizing that the night before
I must have drank too much.

SCOTT ALDERSON

Job Search

I walked inside an office
looking for a job,
the secretary told me
to go and talk to Bob
talk to Bob about the job.

Sorting through the hallway mess
I found Bob behind his desk
sipping on martinis and Triple Sec.

Big fat cow
with hemorrhoids on his ass,
everyone could tell
that he is upper-class.

He told me to fill out an application form
and then pull up a chair,
do not chew your fingernails
and do not mess up your hair.

"What is your job history
how did you do in school
do you have a vehicle
you insignificant fool?"

"Our time is now concluded
you will be notified within the week,"
but no one phoned
no one phoned.

Job Hunt During Recession

Drop resume
fill out application,
standard grand and toy form.

Interview,
jacket and tie:
hair cut short
cologne on chin
neck choked.

Qualifications,
none.
Desires,
food on table
money in bank
no Ferrari
maybe Sherman tank.

Training unavailable
pay below norm
benefits none
poverty since I was born.

Food bank my provider
anger
disillusionment
escape?
Somehow.

5

What If ?

What if?
Death did not occur
deserts were fertile.
Oceans and lakes were cleaned up
poverty did not exist
would the hungry peasant-child sup?

What if?
Atom was never split
banana never peeled
milk not drained from cow
World suddenly brought to peace
tell me Lord
tell me how.

What if?
Computers all broke down
candles had no wicks
hockey was played with baseball bats
instead of wooden sticks.

What if?
Telephones did not ring
and birds did not sing
radios were silent
would death be imminent?

What if?
Everyone was happy?

Untitled

Did your politician tell you
that he loved you
before he raped you of your income,
sodomized your family life
spilled nuclear waste upon your welcome mat,
kissed your baby,
and slapped your wallet on its behind
And told you of reform and referendums
that you found to be harsh and unkind
Did he sell you on the system
and your human rights
sought did he not
the secret
to whom politicians fuck at night.

SCOTT ALDERSON

Three Small White Mice Travelling at the Speed of Light

Decadence in the Inner City

The smell of decay
permeates from dark alleyways
prostitutes and pimps
litter the curbs.

Rain runs down the gutters
a drunk with wetbrain stutters
addicts shoot up then down
businessmen crack from the strain
living in rush mode.

Love and laughter
confined to the
living room
despair and desolation
snorting the cocaine spoon.

Organized crime
disorganized government
biblical prophecy comes true
I am scared
so are you.

Television

Mindless hypnosis,
fantasy becomes leisure
reality escaped,
couch potato
potato chips
time to vegetate.

Brilliant rainbow
channel signed off
loud boisterous advertisements
why don't they just ____ off.

Starving children
in untouchable lands
victims of war
at the hands of man.

Typhoons and volcanoes
eruptions of the times
and Western civilizations
pretending life is fine.

Addicts making news
gays invade the pews
and the churches
suck the peasant dry
in the typhoon reigns.

9

Three Small White Mice Travelling at the Speed of Light

Middle-class suburbanites
Entertainment Tonight
Star Trek and Lost in Space
how did I ever get trapped
in this wretched place?

Dogs of Bureaucracy

Nipping at your feet
devouring you like meat
they are the dogs of bureaucracy,
their system of hierarchy will
tear the flesh from your bones
they just foreclosed on your home.

Leaping down upon you
like maggots drawn to steak
as soon as you fuck up,
they will see what they can take.

Giving orders,
establishing borders,
power struggles in the ranks
embezzling from foreign banks
isn't working fun.

Labour disputes
pregnant employees who have to puke
vacations, vacations, holiday pay
boss, I feel sick today.

SCOTT ALDERSON

#

My dog will no longer go for walks with me
excrete waste in my backyard
bark at the flyer delivery boy
my dog is no longer mine.

My stepson will no longer say no to me
kick and scream because he does not want
to go to bed
tell me that he loves me
or call me Dad;
my stepson is just a memory inside my head.

My wife will no longer make love with me
tell me that she cares
dine with me in paradise
no longer will we share.

Pieces of paper
lock and unlock once-connected souls
lawyers battle in courtrooms
Judges ejaculate judgements
upon old lovers wounds.

Divorce is hell.

Pin Stuck into a Balloon

Head swelling
red corpuscles
profusely exaggerated
sweat
dry mouth
bad breath.

Depression deep
scream without sound
isolation
party favours laid out
circus clowns.

Loneliness
desperation
clinging to life
rope breaking
where will I land.

Eat me alive
taste good?

Cannibals of caring
eating emotions
causing commotion
cataclysm of despair.

Nothing good
most things wrong
death.

SCOTT ALDERSON

Day

8:00 a.m.
liquid filtered
poured into mug
toothpaste
spilled from tube
cap left off;
multivitamins
for multitude of problems
pills for thrills
environmentally safe
like the tampons
under the bathroom sink.

9:00 a.m.
Clothes on
radio on
morning show
news of the day
victims in foreign countries
lay motionless in city streets
children with big bellies
hungry for meat.

9:30 a.m.
brain dead.

10:00 a.m.
more liquid
talk show on T.V.
Donna who?
Hypnotized
morally sodomized

Three Small White Mice Travelling at the Speed of Light
in the invisible air.

12:00 p.m.
Opera with me is on
real estate agent turned millionaire
making money off of other's despair
entertainment or what?

1:00 p.m.
soaps with no mention of soap
who's screwing who?
Lunch for potatoes
potatoes for lunch.

5:00 p.m.
Star Trek
Mr. Spock my hero
emotionless and logical
analytical and cynical
fact not fiction
no hormonal drive
till the mating season
every 7 years
no drugs
no beer
Must be more to life.

SCOTT ALDERSON

Love's Fall from Grace

Love fell from grace
like a speared sparrow
wailing in pain
as it spirals downwards.

Love fell from grace
the skyscraper crumbled
as the earthquake
hit the heart fast.

Remains,
emptiness
void
black hole
walking corpse.

Injury,
no band-aid found
no Lanacane ointment for broken hearts
no elbow pads around.

Love fell from grace
and no one gave a damn
safety and security
gone with the wham.

Love fell from grace
like a dead eagle
caught in the branches of a tree
love fell from grace
the dead eagle is me.

Typing in Head

Keys being punched
paper defaced
headache in brain
miserable place.

Rock on radio
light on in corner
room filled with smoke
coffee in cup
remainder on coffee warmer.

Eyes going out of focus
paper moving
from side to side
some kind of hocus-pocus.

Single spaces
author is in
outerspace
observing from ship.

Machine hums
electricity pouring in
frustration and aggravation
creative sin.

SCOTT ALDERSON

Three Small White Mice Travelling at the Speed of Light

Poem created
brain sedated
craving excitement
in every form.

Sleep time
nursery rhyme
Sung by friend
the end.

Argument # Who Knows

Illusion of love shattered
suffering loss of self-control
you could not leave well-enough alone
you felt you had to be bold.

So I kiss you on the cheek
you spit on my face
saliva dripping down my nose
as per usual, I suffer disgrace.

The crossbow of disaster
shot an arrow through my soul
even the warmth of your love
could not close the hole.

So close the door behind me
I will not be home tonight
another useless arguments
another useless fight.

I pulled the blade from inside of me
made my stand, painful as it was
but instead of just letting go
you had to make a fuss.

Others tried to warn me
of the proven loss of grace
but I closed my eyes
thinking that you were just another victim
of the sadistic human race.

SCOTT ALDERSON

Orgasm Finishes Before It Has A Chance to Start

Two silhouettes embrace under a well-lit sunrise

dancing insanely
making love in the dew stained grass.

Tumbling about in hysterical pleasure
observant of each other's hearts pumping fast
successful in the moment
orgasm finishes before it has a chance to start.

Liquid fills the flesh filled caverns
vocalization fills the air
labouring hands grasped the buttocks
lips become entangled in hair.

The body thrown into seizure-like convulsions
rapid heartbeats suddenly calm
two exhausted entities
disengage their passion psalm.

Through it all they questioned
did the actor suit the part
in traditional relationships
orgasm finishes before it has a chance to start.

Three Small White Mice Travelling at the Speed of Light

Leaving the theatre
having seen through the plot,
two sexually caring Homo Sapiens
become enraged by what they saw.

So, at home
behind the barely-closed door,
two real-life silhouettes
secrete movement on the carpeted floor.

As minutes changed to hours
and rapid pulses continued from their hearts
two sexually caring humans have proven
that orgasm doesn't have to finish before it has a chance to start.

SCOTT ALDERSON

Test Tube Baby

Insertion of flesh softly into
the moistened arena of human birth.

Scientists delight in reproduction
white seed of Homo Sapien
in glass tube.

Passion and love no more
touch removed
soul lock not required
babies made in test tubes.

Morbid

Fingers grip a crumbled corpse
erosion evident
remains of a forgotten past.

Refuse throw into fire
corpses memory
tales of talent.

No funeral today
corpse laid to rest
mislead being
led to death.

Fire burns savagely
sparks soar
nothing remains
only foul smoke
ashes.

I weep
I am the corpse
my past dealt with
surviving death
rebirth.

SCOTT ALDERSON

Do Not Disturb

At times when space is empty
and you are alone and unoccupied
"Do Not Disturb" is your sign
and your walls are fortified.

Boredom is the illusion,
mind bending solitude;
the army's solution to instigate the war
and blow up your home.

No more do not disturb
now you are a front line casualty
caught red-handed in uniform
laughing at the child you have killed.

Villages and towns left in rubble
as the bulldozer of benevolence got boring
so you grabbed the disguise of dictatorship
to wreak Satan's will upon the scarred planet's face.

Oh, Moses where are you now?
With Earth-shattering news of God's word
where is the talking burning tree?
All I see is the fire of system evil
burning in the hearts of humans.

But, alas, there's a sign upon my door
proud and loud
I'll not be a system whore
just do not disturb.

Prepare for Battle

War, pestilence, and famine have been released
upon the scarred planet's face,
bringing the foreseen destruction
of the mindless human race.

Satan's system brings the holocaust into your home,
it's on your TV, it's influencing the person you're talking to
on your telephone.

So grasp the sword of Gideon, the armour of Jehovah,
and prepare for battle my comrade
for the biggest war of all is to come
bigger than any World War.

More devastating than anything that Saddam Hussein and Hitler
combined could have done;
in the effort to cleanse the world of Pagan people
to bring about the paradise once promised
on the sermon on the mount.

Babylon is soon to fall
just like the Berlin Wall.

Truth is freedom but the price is high.

SCOTT ALDERSON

So Few See It

Dancing waves upon the river,
trees dropping their leaves,
a baby's first word,
the first blade of grass to appear in spring time.
Some of the free pleasures of this world.

Making love,
spiritual consciousness,
a cold drink on a hot day,
a warm drink on a cold day.

A nice melody
a relaxing walk in the park
the chirping of a bird in the morning.

The beauty of a robin
the colours of the magpie
the view of the mountains
the sound of a rambling brook.

So beautiful is the world
yet so few see it.

Help

Locked in a closet
of the mind,
making love
to a cold wall,
calling you
calling anyone,
help…

Paranoid
being attacked
parasites feasting
attempting escape
I struggle
I fall,
help…

Intense
Key does not fit
I unlock
I crumble
help…

Losing emotion
blood flows
injury
escape finally
help…

SCOTT ALDERSON

This Planet Would Live

Some people
lack honesty
with
themselves
others
everyone
but,
this as with most
obstacles
can be overcome.

Some people
claim to love
but do they?
love themselves
and everything
everyone?

The answer provides an outcome
if everyone even someone
loved,
then maybe
there would be no hate.

Three Small White Mice Travelling at the Speed of Light

Life instead of death
missiles destroyed
Ozone layer repaired
slaughtering of animals ended
borders taken down.

Maybe
if people loved
this planet would live.

SCOTT ALDERSON

The World

Political sea around us
waves of power
from the elitist state.
Capitalism, Socialism, Communism,
Democracy, Anarchy, Conspiracy
merely soup
to regurgitate.

Swim in the sea
drown.
Peasants die
while class struggles grow
red verses stars and stripes
nuclear weapons
detonate to provide
a worldwide glow.

Many talk of peace
what about unemployment
those who make the bombs
welfare time?

Talk is cheap
peace the sales pitch
unattainable in this system.

Lies mask truth,
Feminism masks equal rights
Chauvinism excuses ignorance
mass murderers are let free
as overcrowded prisons
make the Catholics scream for penance.

Religion long ago lost reason
papal sexual abuse and exploitation
the United Church not united
disagreeing on homosexual ordination
and the sheep will not pay the church's bills.

Prostitution, exploitation, and disintegration
of everyone and everything
personal and business
may as well try not to sink.

All are equal
or so the fallacy goes
reality is segregation
based on how much money one owes.
Food wars, gas wars
and humans actually talk of peace
the warrior race seems to be perishing
as love died on planet Earth
for the system was responsible
for laying the funeral wreath.

SCOTT ALDERSON

The 1988 Olympics

Modern buildings sit on their dirt perches
pillars of concrete their feet
wind moving red and white leaf flags
as if they were weeping.

So empty as the wind without you
caressing me on this balcony of desire.

Nation upon nation turns up
observing the sky for fireworks
shot down in flames.

Closing ceremonies
and the flags are taken down
and the tanks did not follow
the peace games came to town.

My apartment was decorated
for the Babylonians to feast
conquest with gold medal
victory to say the least.

My building exploded
a terrorist had the wrong address
I was left stranded with no home
a victim of an Olympic mess.

The flags no longer danced in the restless wind.

Religious Debate

How many humans have died
under the symbol of the cross?
Hundreds, thousands, maybe millions
took this symbol as their boss.

Compare the cross with the Holocaust.

Christians killing
Commandments covered over
interpretation interesting
killing to preserve
laws that they go against
makes no sense.

Hitler persecuted Jews
and non-Aryans,
Christians
do not discriminate
Jew, non-Aryan
it does not matter
they kill Aryans two.

Holy wars not so holy.

Freedom of religion
freedom to inflict values
on everyone else.

True Christians do not kill
regardless of the reason
so decided by Politicians.

Jesus died for your sins, society, not mine.

SCOTT ALDERSON

Abuse

Like a knife cutting into exposed flesh,
a child's scream pierces the quiet room.
"Please don't touch me there, Daddy"
all that she can speak.

Filled with anger
and sick desire
he instigates incest
and says he loves her
while in daylight
he says he hates her
and comments on her buttocks and breasts.

Daytime comes
time to go to school
where unaware classmates
wonder why she reads so many books
and does not participate
in class discussions nor sports
and in Home Economics,
she refuses to even cook.

Years pass and the abuse is abundant
her Mother worries about her daughter's
mental health.

Mommy picks up the phone
A 1-800 number is dialled
child abuse hotline volunteer
hears the horror for the first time.

Two weeks later,
a textbook Social Worker visits
Daddy is not home
a case is made
policemen take Daddy away
only to let him go
the very next day.

One year later
the daughter kills herself
her only way out
so she thought.

Mommy shoots Daddy
now she serves the life term.

Why didn't anyone listen to the little girl?

SCOTT ALDERSON

Halloween

Children converge on the streets as night time nears,
armed with grocery bags they greet their peers.
Dressed in costumes, make-up on their face
anxious for the candy taste.

Parents panic at home
· scared that Junior might get mugged
supper for scum on the streets
junior gets hugged.

Wearing a mask, a stranger approaches junior
promising candy for a ride in his car
the police should have come sooner.

Junior went for the ride
his parents nearly died
when Junior did not come home
his baby sister cried.

Junior's body was found three days later
floating motionless in a pond,
another Halloween
come and gone.

Making Love in a Rain Forest

Vines dangle from moistened branches
of monolithic trees
the animals cry out in estrangement;
man has invaded
woman has invaded.

Two beings make bizarre physical motions
on the forest floor.

SCOTT ALDERSON

Listening to a Loved One Crying

Tears echo like raindrops hitting a window
from the once-silent room
now filled with despair.

I am apart
I cannot offer help.

You cry
I cry too.

Pain sears my skin
your pain shows in my eyes.

I try to comfort
but don't fulfil

I am sorry.

Sniffles and wetness continue.

A War of Understanding

Bold lines on an empty page
singing to the madman;
signalling the start
a war of understanding
to end it would be a waste.

Everything is empty
the paper, the cupboards, my life
mostly
my soul.

Bold sunrise on a dark horizon
alarm clock for the dead,
signalling the start
a war of understanding
to end it would extinguish life.

Everything is lies
the country, the society, my speech
mostly
life as I know it.

Bold time for an empty man
speaking to the world;
signalling the beginning of decomposition
a war of understanding
to end it would bring hope.

SCOTT ALDERSON

Three Small White Mice Travelling at the Speed of Light

Everything can be wonderful
life, the universe, existence
mostly
my small world.

Enough

Like a child
I let you play
like an actress
I let you act
but in the final outcome of the day,
it is you who plunges a knife into my back.

Like a mate
I comfort you through sorrow
like a barbarian
I defend your honour
pride gets in the way of tomorrow
and your ego covers me with dishonour.

Age becomes the nightmare
sexuality the tigers-trap
existence in an affair
brains splattered on my lap.

So I ramble in ludicrous accusations
to further seal the crevice of my heart
to prevent my own annihilation
the time has come for me to depart.

So I retreat into isolation
to formulate my thoughts
and without me on this desert of desolation
I think you would be better off.

SCOTT ALDERSON

Three Small White Mice Travelling at the Speed of Light

So I leave you with no harmony behind
no memory of me sensitive and kind
just a love full of fear
a love too hard to contend with
a constant pain in my rear.

Amnesiac

Do you remember childhood?
Or was it stolen
some evil committed against your person
leaving you amnesiac.

Was it your dad who ruined you?
dear old dad's favourite drink
personality change
demon's released from inside
attacking defenceless you.

Did your mother try to protect you?
only to be slapped around
and in a moment of sobriety
was an apology for inexcusable behaviour
offered by the circus clown.

Physician heal thyself
regain your spiritual wealth
try not to be a victim all your life
and regain your mental health.

Time For An Alias

Sitting in darkness
not by choice I might add
power company the new enemy
bill not paid for months
now my credit is bad.

Candle companion
cooking on gas stove
separate account for gas
probably will be shut off
next week with the money I owe.

Food reserves no longer reserved
like a busy restaurant
my reservation has been cancelled
taxman seized my refund
guess he needed it more than I.

Court date notice came in the mail
why do they call it a date?
A date is what single people wish for
so maybe I'll forfeit mine
to someone more deserving
someone lonely for recognition.

Is it time for an alias
An AKA for the once known as
the peasant reborn
to acquire new riches
under a pseudonym
death via the system.

Naked in his Rotted Cage

Copyright 1995

Authors Note – This work is dedicated to my Mom, Kevin, Linda, Sandra, Sharon, Rich, Cam, Rein and all my other family and friends.

Imagination must run wild
for if not
we begin the disintegration
to the death-like state of
normalcy and conformity of the mind.

Bio

Born in Edmonton, Alberta, Canada in 1964 now residing in Calgary, Alberta. The youngest of five, Scott began writing poetry at 18 years of age as songs to be performed by a band. Music has always been a major influence and inspiration. Scott writes on themes of politics, economics, introspection and human sexuality. With his second book, *Naked in his Rotted Cage*, he attempts to further enlighten readers to the many realms of modern poetry. It is for you the reader that this is given.

The poem "Naked in his Rotted Cage" is also published in the anthology "Island Sunsets" through the Poetry Institute of Canada, 1995.

Shoelaces Left Untied

Bronze bodies exchange glances
on concrete pathways
smiling, waving
only to collide
bruised knee
broken teeth
shoelaces left untied
the large oak tree
from whence they fell beneath
became disenchanted
a muffled groan
no pleasure dome
and they both walked away.

Another day came the chance
to greet again
nodding, winking
only to dance
stepped on toes
a broken nose
shoelaces left untied
the tiled floor
the exit door
from whence they left together
closed abruptly
an alarmed look
fate took
and they both walked away
together and yet alone.

SCOTT ALDERSON

Telephone Ringing Off Its Perch

Silence can be greatness
if only to last a while
escape from stimulation
overwhelming
and overrated
busy streets
sore feet
from traversing the tapestry
of modern life.

Computer output
printer activated
telephone ringing off its perch
fax machine beeping
paper tray empty
boss screaming bloody murder
secretaries week next week.

Television left on for hours
dinner dishes piled in sink
Neighbours fighting
dog shit on front lawn
telephone ringing off its perch
solicitors banquet
furnace cleaning
carpet cleaning
list goes on and on.

So, silence can be greatness
if only to last a while
escape from stimulation
climb down
from the shit pile.

SCOTT ALDERSON

We Die So You Can Live

Like Gods the Poets ask to be heard
only to bear scrutiny from all.

With figures of speech as our tools
rhythm, rhyme, and reason as our rules
we write to free inside thought.

With promises of better tomorrow's
free of pain and never-ending sorrows
we die so you can live.

Adulterer

Lipstick
smeared on a collar
perfume
scent on a neck
tattered clothes
messy hair
yet innocence
is the plea.

Phone rings
hang up
letter in the mail
hugs and kisses
signature smeared with blush
unexpected business trip
reservation for two
pantyhose found in suitcase.

Innocence
cheap word from the guilty
late night at work
open door
visit by mate
caught in the act
penetration with permission
forced to fornicate.

SCOTT ALDERSON

Naked in his Rotted Cage

> Deceiver
> non-believer
> lies mask the guilt
> bottom of the pile
> of shit and filth.

Naked In His Rotted Cage

Since time began
the peasant ran
to survive
yes, to merely thrive
within the corrupted world.

Sold his wares
and no one cared
if he died
or if he cried
naked in his rotted cage.

Now the lottery calls
dreams of freedom windfalls
if he won
he'd come undone
crushing creditors necks.

Buy a ticket
before you get sickened
by the reality
and the mentality
of this system.

SCOTT ALDERSON

Through A Dream

Through a dream
the vision came
empty, hollow
eyes focused staring
through a thin glass pane.

Screams of a child
pierced the quiet night
stirred by insanity
sitting up in bed
awakened by the fright.

Tears splashing
on a naked cheek
calming words from a loved one
plugging up the leak.

Return to coma-like status
closed eyelids twitching
in the dark room
and animal sounds echo
from an open mouth.

I Remember

I remember childhood
and wishing the demon would die
school halls full of false dreams
home hollow with alcoholic lies.

I remember opening Christmas presents
like Barbarians at a pig roast
tearing and slashing little peasants
deeply engulfed in pagan bliss.

I remember fear as my captor
terror my best friend
loneliness my lover
hell, the demons den.

I remember the herb seducing me
as the needle lures the junkie in
medication for open wounds
preventing outsiders from seeing in.

I remember institution
hotel lacking casino
school without bells
hospital without emergency.

I remember recovery
most of all,
I remember my humanity.

SCOTT ALDERSON

I Feel Like A Puppy

I feel like a puppy
in a pet store window
waiting to be purchased.

Loser, winner
waiting for the bidder
on the sinner.

Like meat on a hook
I rot in my own juices
tearing me apart.

The butcher cut me.

I was packaged at birth
infant in plastic wrap
awaiting destiny to spill misery
onto my virgin lap.

There are those who admire
several even desire
yet, at what cost?

How much is this puppy in the window?

Writing Is The Same

If I described a car to you
would you wonder in my choice of words?
Would you ponder my intentions
of writing so elegantly in a non-elegant world?

If I rhymed a line
or wasted time
would I capture your attention
with my pen of redemption?

Would you or will you
label my tone
style and diction
to compare me to the fool
or strip me to the bone?

Am I connotative, denotative
or merely insane
far as I can see,
analysis is a pain.

What's my theme
what do I mean?
Maybe society will label me
a sick, demented fiend.

Free verse, blank verse
writing is the same
in seeking enlightenment for the reader
knowledge is the purpose to be gained.

SCOTT ALDERSON

Burn-Out From Education

Burn-out from education
disintegration
degradation
of positive energy within my mind.

History shuns me with disbelief
as people have been out of control
the weak and the bold
fighting for the real estate unsold.

Yes,
we are warriors
combatants on paper
literary mercenaries
with thoughts of enlightenment
for the human mind.

The artist pleas for sanity
in the insane reality
in which the world exists
yet the stockpiling of weapons
hunger and merciless deaths
in the deadened system still persists.

So speak to me Creator
your sheep flocked off
and never returned to the field
destined through ignorance
to fester disease, death, and decay
and demolish free will.

SCOTT ALDERSON

Fade, Fade Away...

Fade, fade away young man
hibernate to become aware,
make the day much brighter
say a prayer for the World.

Light a candle for the deceased
wear a poppy
kill the communists
before they take control.

Legion alcoholics hold ceremonies
acknowledging the fact that they could be six feet under
with maggots engulfing their parasitic corpses
so they thank Christ and drink to remember.

Salute the flag young man
your country needs you
to kill fellow humans
be the proud, the few, the Vietnam fuck-ups.

Be prepared
for tomorrow
politics becomes more
end to a beginning that never was
life taken for real estate
property foreclosed.

Remember, but lest we forget
yes, everyone else has
have we really progressed?

Home Sweet Home

Watching grass grow
walls melting to close me in
thick film of mould
on the milk
used to coat my cereal.

Clothes piled in the laundry hamper.

Some call me slob
place not fit for dogs
home sweet home.

Driveway lacking cars
windows without bars
deadbolt alive.

Green dishes
dust balls in the corner
coffee grounds weeks old
wilted lettuce in fridge
bathtub married to scum
frayed wires from the lamp
home sweet home.

SCOTT ALDERSON

Fever

Head swollen
like after a two week pot binge
body cold
mental hypothermia
forehead
like the river Styx.

Illusion
pill to cure
relief
normalcy
complacency
like a Koala in a tree.

Dizzy
itchy
bugs crawling on my skin
feast or famine
when will it end?

Streetwalker [for Tina]

I knew you once
a shattered image of childhood dreams
lost, confused, and abandoned
grasping at wealth by any means.

Victim of society
social outcast on welfare
empty fridge and barren cupboards
truly I cared.

Now you stroll the path
highway to despair
to be a shattered image of adulthood
letting pimps rule your lair.

And, as months become years
The hunter sets his bait
you will walk the evening stroll
believing that men
are the people you should hate.

So now I only smile
as I pass you on the street
memories splattered against a mirror
reflection of the person you used to be.

SCOTT ALDERSON

Hardening of the Arteries

Sometimes I wish I'd never been born.
Thrown into a nuclear age
where pain and cruelty
dominate in a superficial falsity
known as society.
Humanistic...... bullshit.

And the light of day cracks the dawn,
carrying a snickering smile,
and I laugh at the scene,
but the moment remains for nothing.

And I scream forth
the blistering obscenities of my life.

We merely exist
particles within a mass
unaware and uninformed,
we allow others to lead us to our death
the Moral Majority.

And I cry to you,
to a deaf God within a deaf sky,
and I say, "Why do you even listen with the power to shatter eternity?"
But when the echoes die,
the mass quivers in fear,
at the loss of hope.

My soul shatters as I approach the Dead Zone,
inflicted upon my being.
The mind caresses the shards of my life.
A broken mirror of false reality
oh woe be the picture of pain.
And you who travel the slippery night
do not step across the crimson stain,
to reach reality.

SCOTT ALDERSON

Naked in his Rotted Cage

The Horror of Babylon, the Violence of Rome

I do not understand the world
or maybe I understand it too well
how did we ever come so far?
yet never leave home
the horror of Babylon, the violence of Rome.
Empires wielding leaders
militant became the norm
rules, policies, and procedures
to make the peasant conform.
Priests and Politicians in bed together
making hate.

Chemical, nuclear, and germ warfare
and the machine calls its master to be enslaved.

Lessons in history
supposed deterrent to repetition
society looks for scapegoats
to deny responsibility
one person is to blame
so the fallacy goes.

But Hitler, Stalin, and Mussolini combined
did not kill as many
as do their followers of reason
and the Machiavellian puppets
society elects.

Isms represent the problem
labelling does not solve them
as we continue under the doomsday clock
and await our Creator.

SCOTT ALDERSON

False Dreams
and
Realities

I awaken
from a beautiful dream
to face the nightmare of life,
no money, no home
no wife.

So I cry in bereavement
at the harsh reality unfolded under glazed eyes.
In the end it does not help
in the beginning it merely felt
like I was out of my mind.
Bruises now appear on my once delicate skin.

The future tempts me
like a donkey led by a carrot on a stick.
Powerless I stumble blindly in the real world.
Conformity and repression
drug abuse and depression
symptoms.
They tell me things are different across the Gospel fence
belief brings harmony and thus I'll be content
to lead my peasant existence in a commercialized world
of false dreams and realities.

The Inside Cracking of Their Clay

I close my eyes
exquisite visions of beauty
disrupt the darkness
a voice calls out my name
it is you seeking an answer
to cure the insecurity
of a coupled future.

I wake to reassure
and suggest we seek Utopia
and run through fields of ceramic figurines
avoiding the insane cracking of their clay
watch with me the world crumbling
united we shall shape our world, our way.

SCOTT ALDERSON

Crumbling Within Chaos

Crumbling within chaos
babbling within a brook
cast away by the current
caught up in the strife.

Lost my home
wasted by tornado
carpet needed cleaning
money was not there.

System sucked me dry
as the wind blew through my hair
winter chill without wisdom
cupboards lay bare.

What Say You ?

What seen you
as the gaze was cast
into the staring mirror?
Did the reflection
scare you into psycho?
world captured in fear.
Did you smile?
As the executioner's blade
sliced through years of
anguish and agony
silent tears.
What say you
now is the empty
is reality?
Wish you were here
to see what is left behind
the closure of a chapter
the treasurer left to find
so seek you;
the wise one
leads you from negative,
retrieve the bounty
for fortune awaits.

SCOTT ALDERSON

Forward

Doves hover above me
whispering greetings.

Trees bend with the wind
allowing my passage.

The path widens
salamanders race across.

No dead end ahead
no fence to stop me.

Forward.

Season Spits Venom

Been dozens of days
since the smile awoke
to glaze my face.

Like moss to a rock
frowns appear in mass
a shattered complexion.

Crow's feet infect my eyes
age of maturity
locked in stifled anxiety.

The season spits venom
cursing cold and cabin fever
flu-like mental calamity.

Within these walls we played
and danced without glory
now only tears remain
splashing quietly off plant leaves.

SCOTT ALDERSON

#

Armies of spruce trees
line the horizon
Geese play in the pond
safe from plane engines and guns
injured by stray white balls.

Flags mark the hole
the Capitalists deal is sewn
carts buzz by like a congested freeway
fore means duck.

Caddy is the grunt
weighed down by circumstance
holding the bag
for the money dance.

Caresses of the Mind

Multicolour spectrum visual
upon introduction
world moving
in slow motion
no problems
penniless
but happy
riding transit bus.

New language created
score me this
hit me with that
Rasta man creation
God in a joint
big bust
Cop kicked in my door
bars now hold me
my freedom is ignored.

SCOTT ALDERSON

Naked in his Rotted Cage

Untitled

Animal sounds
echo from behind a closed door
bed springs
stretched beyond safe limits.

Isolation via passion
world remedy with relief
slow pace without end.

SCOTT ALDERSON

I Found the Light Switch

Struggled through darkness
to find the light switch
buried under clothes
carelessly discarded by the owner.

Rambled incessantly
about hardship and injustice
paid the piper
and kicked him in the groin.

Fought hand to hand
with monotony and boredom
to reach the plateau of competition
only to lose the battle.

Sought peace and serenity
within a war obsessed society
only to be captured
and put into a concentration camp.

Broke free through the wall
independent thoughts returned
I found the light switch
buried under clothes
carelessly discarded by the owner.

SCOTT ALDERSON

College Disqualification

Saw the pillar protruding
from ground level
swerved around it
with the speed and cunning
of a squirrel avoiding traffic.

Squished a pop can
on my journey
ready to recycle
the obvious garbage
of having gone astray.

Knocked on the door
of future opportunity
only to be turned away
by what could have been
what might have been.

Teachers taught me poverty
student loan taught me debt
default and denial
and no certificate
diploma dead before birth.

Enlightenment

With an enlightened mind
comes added responsibility
and yet survival
is the goal.

Reality,
love is non-compatible
with our warrior society
of competition and egocentrism.
Dependency,
new word for caring;
sex the dreaded disease
Bureaucrats and Politicians
nothing more than common thieves.

The Clergy class is corrupt
immorality the new mentality
leaders lacking conscience
sucking life out of the walking dead.
Spousal abuse and enslavement
has become the norm
statistics reflect the horror
it's enough to make one vomit.

What went wrong in the plan for a Utopian World?

SCOTT ALDERSON

Reflection on Spring

Leaves discarded by trees
Summers end once again
death, like the absence of a smile
on the admirer's face
vacant, abandonment
non-creative loss of grace.

What deed removed the smile?
Was it the same as killed the trees?
Is it lack of love and happiness
has this afflicted thee?

Spring arrives
green buds signal the awakening
of the sleepy-eyed trees
but the smile failed to return
to the admirer's face
as he filled his being with darkness
slave to a system
focussed on death.

Political Love Letter

Why dost thou lie so much
oh large figure filling my television screen?
Is it glory and praise thou seek
from the suit man engrossed in money.
Does not the commoner's plight concern you
as they ferret the garbage bin
for their daily bread?
Does not concern for your electorate's survival
as your economic cutbacks slash them
play upon your conscience in your head?

And yet you smile oh great leader
as your party pillages the peasant
kicking him in the groin.
Like dirty knickers worn for weeks
your policies on reform stink
all this crap to save some coin.
Oh when will it end exalted leader
worshipped as the Capitalists God?
When will you finally end up on welfare
and become the fisherman's cod?

SCOTT ALDERSON

Or So The Fallacy Goes

What carnage awaits
on the road ahead?
What blockades must I hurdle
what curves must I bend?
in order to find rest stop
from the wrath of debtors unquenched
by mere empty promises
and pleas for mercy
while endeavouring restitution
unlike monetary prostitution
or so the fallacy goes.

Yet I seek a higher knowledge
for without I plummet
metres to the edge
and the system heralds the trumpet
as the rebel dies
a quiet death
without glory
just debts left behind
clocks left to wind
no battle cry for righteousness
or so the fallacy goes.

Maybe Today

Maybe today we'll make a dollar
two if we're lucky
enough for Ichiban and wieners
can't afford to be fussy.

Someone benefitted from my benefit check
probably some Bureaucrat
with empty pockets
paid handsomely to act.

Theatre of the absurd
voice echoing turds
rabbit pellets of thought
shit solutions
for economic dissolution
inside the Canadian mosaic.

A collage of labelling
and studies of the problem
while we starve and thirst
with dreams as our companion.

Maybe today we'll make a cake
top it with lottery tickets
and dreams of the bungalow
two cars in the driveway surrounded by white pickets.

SCOTT ALDERSON

Acknowledgements

I wish to thank the following for their inspiration in the writing of this work: All those in my sphere of influence, Pink Floyd, Capitalism for its constant pain on the poor, Politicians for messing up the world, children for their innocence, my Mom for my birth, my teachers for their encouragement especially Cindy Hudson my English 30 teacher, poets of days gone by and to come, and last but certainly not least, you the reader for you give life to this paper.

Scott Alderson

Reflective Energies

Copyright 1996

This work is dedicated to me. Special thanks to all those involved in the production and imaginative process towards the completion of this work.

When you peer out your window what do you see?

SCOTT ALDERSON

Reflections

Looked deep into a cracked mirror
splintered by the past
saw a handicapped shadow
poised like a statue
returning my gaze.

Attempted shaving, inflicted a wound
slit skin
bandaged
looked for my chair
to wheel myself away.

Got lost in my bathroom
found the toilet
flushed my misery
the reflection remained
the cracked mirror reassembled.

Stopped staring as if by request
wandered aimlessly for days
found a different mirror
saw my reflection,
the handicapped man walked.

Feel free, left without burden
no shadow, no slit skin
no chair needed
reflections of my being
mirror within.

Anger Swells

Anger swells
like a helium balloon loading
suddenly it blows up
ferocious and foreboding.

What began the process?
was it poverty not pleasantry
was it life's little stresses
now what to do?

Vent or keep contained
action versus reaction
oh the strain, of living gets me down.

The tiger roars
screaming lunacy under the moon
Antelopes anticipate death
and run radically into the brush.

No one was hurt
while release was achieved
the balloon burst
peace was once again conceived.

SCOTT ALDERSON

For Eileen

Sleep now second Mother
your rest is well deserved;
of perseverance and long-suffering
some of the lessons we have learned.

Those of us left awake
bear the scars of loneliness
memories our new companion
our love again confessed.

So sleep now second Mother
your years of pain have ceased
rest quietly dear one
until again we meet
in the promised paradise.

The Man Once Only a Boy

When I was young
innocent and having fun
life seemed so exciting
dangerous and inviting.

As I grew
I somehow knew
the toys would change
to suit the adult game.

The cars, the bars, the wars
all seemed to me so far
from my extended reach
just like Jamaica's beach.

Dope drained the dreams
looking back so it seemed
and yet so much I learned
how to survive and not get burned.

New dreams in middle-age
yet to accomplish, on life's stage
new toys, new games, new joys
the man once only a boy.

SCOTT ALDERSON

Snowflake Ballet

A snowflake
fell from the sky
landing recklessly
in the once vacant chair
now bearing weight.

Pale
yet full of life
laughing with me
over coffee and biscotti.

She melts away
under my hot touch
a moment captured in time
a fantasy while dreaming.

Another winter's eve
and we shall dance again
under the half moon
intoxicated by cold
sobered by coffee.

Inspire Me

Inspire me
with wisdom
and knowledge
stimulate my intellect
I need to learn
I need to grow
I need to live.

Cover me
with blankets of hope
cuddle me
with sheets of honesty
I need to see
I need to hear
I need to exist.

Encourage me
with visions
of beauty
stimulate my intellect
I need to dream
I need to appreciate
I need to survive.

SCOTT ALDERSON

Doing Fine

Ashtray
full of butts
wallet empty
am I not enough?

Goal orientation
lacks in satisfaction
and results in need for medication.

Smoked myself into a coma
clothes saturated with the aroma
of stress
more or less
the cause of death for most
then laid into a coffin
the parasites host.

Emptied ashtray
new day, new dawn
wallet full
still not enough.

Reality orientation
lacks in satisfaction
like mental masturbation.

Quit smoking so as to live
woke up from the coma
sprung to attention to face life's melodrama
of conflict
while the clock ticked
the alarm signalled departure time
so I left in a hurry
I'm okay
I'm doing fine.

SCOTT ALDERSON

Close Encounter

From deep space they came
invited by us via satellite
welcomed in every language known
and every mind feared.

Unknown they watched for decades
studying via abduction
close encounters with two-legged
mostly bags of water.

Ship by ship
they came in mass
alien upon alien
to kick Earth's ass.

With lasers they sought to enslave us
the jungle beast thousands of years
out of his cave with gunpowder
and different brands of beers.

Fire was no defence as the alien attack
just became more and more intense
until like zombies
we were forced to obey them.

The war was over
the aliens had won
and their victory song played
as we said farewell to the Sun.

Day 2

I'm following rainbows,
created by tears of insecurity
hoping to acquire the gold
with the Walkman etching me closer to deafness.

I'm stepping out
freedom from the wheelchair
stretching limbs to achieve motion
while some dickhead is pushing me on a crowded
C-Train.*

I'm moving memories
from past to future tense
not existing in either
yet some ghost keeps giving me goosebumps.

I'm falling into bed
exhausted from the pace
lacking sexual nourishment
while the adult video store is packed.

I'm sleeping now
don't wake me up
till light pierces the Venetian blinds
and lips of silk massage my face.

* C-Train – Light Rail Transit system used in Calgary, Alberta.

SCOTT ALDERSON

Collection Agency

Creditor crawled out of his burrow
like a groundhog, to use his phone
called me casually yesterday
to see if I was home.

Said he wanted wads of green paper
transferred from my wallet to his hands.
He felt rejected by my stubbornness
when I wholly disagreed with his plan.

Threatened legal action shortly
while sending me loads of letters
and spending tonnes of postage
think that he would know better.

Reacted rather viciously
as I refused to play his game
of intimidation and harassment
so the debt remains unpaid.

Called him today at his office
just to see if he was working
I told him what a jerk he had been
and that I was not joking
when I told him to choke on a chicken bone.

The Day the Flowers Came Back to Life

Waves of wind assault me
violating my balance
forcing me to the ground.

As the helicopter lands in the park
flowers in green camouflage clothes
run towards me guns ejaculating
lilies dropping everywhere
I can no longer sit on the fence and grow
I'm front line fodder for the system cops.

My weapon chosen carefully
the truth will defeat the lie
on this day we will be glad
to live as one, to forget the past
the animal, the flower, equal at last.
No nectar drainers just dreams reawakened
roots of mental health to nourish from
no more blind flowers, no more dumb
awakened to kiss the day
the flowers came back to life.

SCOTT ALDERSON

Gas Station

Cars caress concrete
while I watch from a naked field
stripped of bush and tree
no rabbits, no gophers, no deer
only little old me.

I share my space with Shell
the scent of fumes saturate my coveralls
grease embraces my cigarette pocket
my Chevette is angled parked by the car wash
think I remembered to lock it.

Dog hairs flow like a lion's mane.
as they suck air in the back of a pick-up
eighty miles an hour, redneck at the wheel
baseball cap, long hair, and moustache
is this guy for real?

My fuel hose fornicates with the Firebird
topping the tank for the trip
six bucks an hour for all this prestige
job without advancement or benefits
why don't I just leave?

Lonely

I need someone
to join me on life's monorail
to help me build reality
to free some dreams
to live harmoniously
to laugh uncontrollably
to smile in opposition
to cross over juxtaposition
to show courage under stress.

I need someone
to complement the hiking trail
to be hypnotized by the campfire
burning deep within
the passion storm of creative sin.

I need connection
plug me in for a recharge
massage these tense muscles
as together we would share
the miracles of pleasure.

SCOTT ALDERSON

Flood

Nature vomited into my basement
cracked the foundation
making my carpet unhealthy.
I cracked as well
chronic perspiration
as I talked to Mr. Insurance man.
"No coverage," so he said
while my home was liquidated
policies with clauses
so I further equated
Noah and myself to be of kin
yet in different times.

Sandbags only sought to annoy the enemy
my brothers and sisters had littered her for ages
she shook she sought to change my cul-de-sac
from concrete to ocean in a day
as Mr. Insurance man chuckled
"No coverage," so he said
policies with clauses
bankrupt on the river bank
can't pay the company
to pump the water from my house.

Blind

Count my steps
1, 2, 3,
turn right
or is it left?
My cane is broken
spirit alive and well
please do not pity me
I can hear
I can smell.

Darkness is my reality
with the light of hope
as my companion.
My dog guides me
man's best friend
but do not pet him
he is working hard
navigating every bend.

I am blind not stupid
don't shout I can hear
just grasp my hand and lead me
to the edge of the pier.
I wish to smell water
hear wave slashing at wood
imagine the Sun setting silently
on some horizon far away.

SCOTT ALDERSON

Totally Deaf

I see your mouth moving
frustration coats your face
swinging arms for persuasion
waiting for my response.

You seem agitated to be met
by my serene silence
guess they did not tell you
I'm totally deaf.
Talk slower and I'll read
your ruby inflated lips,
or sign into my silence
fingers taking form.

Don't scream
I cannot hear you
please don't push me
to get my attention
I see you
I just can't hear you
I'm totally deaf.

Within

Within shadows
I crawl
leopard removed of spots
bat removed of wings.

Within dreams
I lived
a man lacking creativity
a man void of sensitivity.

Within cities
I thrive
emotionless and empty
a human sacrifice.

Within tears
I am captured
lost and lonely
no vision of escape.

Within evening
I cry
for love's dissolution
for a child's pain.

Within lines on paper
I release
unlocked for healing to begin
past deceased to wash my skin.

SCOTT ALDERSON

Portrait 1

Silhouette gazing,
almost painfully filling
the window frame;
clear eyed and happy
smile
like the rainbow upside down
after a spring rain.

"Smile fresh for the onlookers
beaming life energy
fulfilled like the window frame,
speak novels of poetry to me
while eating grapes
hand fed, of course
drink wine from poised glasses
no second thoughts, no remorse."

Let us speak flippantly
about little things
those lacking meaning
listen to the wrens sing.
Let us walk the beach as one
sand massaging naked feet
let us run through mountain streams
water splashing
like frogs dancing
puddles parted like the red sea
Bambi in the forest for us to meet.

But, alas my lovely
you are just a silhouette
I know not even your name
just a fair maiden gazing
almost painfully filling
the window frame.

SCOTT ALDERSON

Dandelion

Dandelion smiled good morning
for days after the rain came
I got tired of waving back
so I killed them with the WeedEx bar.
I smiled good day at them then
as they curled up like caterpillars
poisoned by the bar like alcohol
gasping only to further inhale.

No longer yellow with an arm toward the Sun
No longer living from a root
just another victim of my wickedness
just another day when I came undone
like the zipper half closed
the stitch once sewn that no longer holds the hem
the belt on the second notch holding up my pants.

Mowed my lawn today
dead dandelions filled the bag
Glad garbage bags of poison
no longer will they smile,
so I frown at the void
pause for a while,
and gloat my success
the WeedEx bar armed
in the garden shed
and me armed as always
deep inside my head.

The Blind

Pulled one down
twisted another
seen my neighbours
copulating on their couch,
TV on
can of beer on the coffee table
cowboy boots on
baseball cap turned around
moving back and forth
while fabric corroded their knees.

Different window, different blind
Seen a street person
cursing and waving hello
with closed fists,
guess he came across gym shorts
when he examined the neighbour's garbage;
pulled one backup
twisted another the other way
closed the blinds.

SCOTT ALDERSON

Remote Control

The VCR ejected me
having played me faithfully for years
with the finesse and formality
of a well-tuned machine.
This device hates me now
no longer plays when the buttons are pushed
just eject, eject, and eject.

No more recordings
no more playback
of those old tapes
we used to rewind
and rarely fast forwarded.
Pause never worked
and stop was always pushed
when it all had ended naturally.

The VCR ejected me
it's head was very dirty
so I grabbed a Q-Tip and alcohol
and moisturized myself
now I seek a divorce
a return to manufacturer
turning in my extended warranty
to get on with my life.

Salty Taste In My Mouth

From a distant ridge
sitting on a jagged rock
watching brothers tear each other apart,
tears infect my eyes.

Violent words from an angry mouth
inflicting wounds not even a surgeon
could possibly seal.

What horror caused this demise?
What virtue is there in insanity?
What's it going to take to be nice?

Time out for kindness
too much evil in this world
too much pain I am observing
from this jagged rock.

I must close my eyes
the salty taste in my mouth
is most unpleasant.

A genesis of healing must occur
some sort of sanity we must procure
in order to get along,
no more middle fingers saluting the masses
somehow we need to teach humanity in our classes
to bring us out of imperfection.

SCOTT ALDERSON

Rambling

Hither yee of ancient lore
hence listen to one so righteously poor.

Thou hast awoke the sleeping spirit
cast aside this many fortnight.

Do not hesitate oh vanity
for ego came before the fall,
trap not this transient
for gratitude is not your treasure
nor love your gratuity.

Hence forth lay down beside me
thou may leave thy oral weapons of destruction
sheathedin your mouth.

I seek not the battle
for today is the day of celebration
that of birth
so seek shelter my suckling
for goodness has landed
thou hast found thy connection.

What Sins Will We Commit?

What realms of passion shall we visit?
What head games will you choose not to play?
What pleases you, making you gasp?
What sins will we commit today?

Bubble baths and champagne
candles burning and soft music
a baby oil massage and making love
keep me from going insane.

Let's just be friends shall we
let's just pretend shall we
let's run naked in the city parks
at dawn in spring before the city wakes.
Let's search the labyrinth of loneliness
the singles bar
to seek out passions from lovers lost
from those people emotionally scarred.

Seek I do
the pleasures of life in abundance
give as I receive I do
allowing smiles to penetrate my hardened face
to make my world more fulfilled
to make my space a desirable place.

SCOTT ALDERSON

Seek the Rhyme

submerged
periscope down
found myself
alone and indifferent
an insect on the grass

drowning
breath gone
found myself
engulfed in chaos
together and apart
senses way off

dreaming
mental sedation
found myself
crucified as Jesus
and so I left
always knew I could

soaring
breath restored
find myself
lonely at times
and so I create
and seek the rhyme

Break Up Number 15

We swam in the pond
tadpoles eager to grow
seeking pads to meditate on.

Siamese twins
surgically separated
now I drown alone.

Consumed to saturation
mosquito filled with blood
now I seek a new nest.

Not hungry for the hive
I seek the flower
nectar, to inspire creativity.

SCOTT ALDERSON

Take Comfort Friend

Sometimes rain comes
even when the sun is shining
but life is too short
to be miserable
too unpredictable
to be ruled by fear.

Sometimes you feel like crying
even though it goes against conditioning
but brainwashing can be overcome
to restore health to an injured spirit

Sometimes it seems as though
everyone and thing is out to get you,
even the toilet has a hidden agenda
as it plugs and then overflows onto your floor.

Sometimes the plunger seems out of reach
or cannot be found in its usual place
but take comfort friend in imperfection
after all,
you are just part
of the human race.

Untitled

I bear not
the fruits of knowledge
this sunny dusk.

I seek no revelation
no act of faith
this body is old.

Lend me your listener
in its canals let me swim
so that I may finally hear
the pleasures from within.

Cast upon me your glance
oh sacred virtue
silken robe of admiration;
this mind is young
these years they listen
let me in.

I walked far today
through the reign of ignorance
to find this sunny dusk
yet I bear thee no fruit.

SCOTT ALDERSON

You'd

You'd like it here
so much potential
walls lacking pictures
yet speaking memories.

You'd put a bow on the door
close the drapes
so as not to see the whores
walking the concrete.

You'd bless this house
with incense and candles
praying for poverty to end
at the fireplace mantle.

You'd clap your hands for me
commendation for survival
and then laugh while walking away
flashing me a tinge of your black bra.

Hope you're happy without me
May life smile upon your face
I'll be okay, I have people who care
and I like my new space.

Don't Answer Only Question

Why do we give power
to object and animals?

Crows and bats
wolves and crosses
bulls and goats
sheep and bosses.

Does the snake
lie on purpose?

Does the dove
represent peace?
Does the swastika
represent intolerance?
What do you represent?

Do you believe in miracles
truth, justice or what?

Don't answer, only question.

SCOTT ALDERSON

Crow

Why does the crow
sing a song of despair?
elegance in black
elegance in flight.

If I could fly
I would visit you,
elegance in white
freedom in flight.

I would sing a song of peace
a song to end all wars
upon your balcony
while my feet grasp cold steel.

I would teach the masses
to think, think, think
to question existence outside themselves
to don another's cloak for a day
to be kind to one another
but, like the crow
I sing a song of despair
elegance in black
elegance to write?

Untitled

On my way to paradise
privileged to dine
with one I cared so much for
didn't cost a dime

caviar was in abundance
candles and flowers
gracing every banquet table
feeling pumped with power

danced decadently in paradise
made love slowly on its beaches
soft mounds of flesh in my mouth
pretty pink peaches.

SCOTT ALDERSON

Keep Me From Going Insane

fighting depression
cause I've been here before
psycho trigger jumping
head banging hardwood floor

burned fingers with the Bic
cause I've been here before
edge of a virtual reality
come on gimmee some more

pierced my eyelid
never done it before
caused pain to reconfirm feelings
previously ignored

so rip off my shirt
peel the onion known as my brain
slash my jugular slightly
to keep me from going insane

lock me up in bondage
of not self not chain
sedate the psycho trigger
remove the nasty stain.

Euthanasia

Who eats, who does not?
Who decides?
Who dictates the fate we've got
Who denies?

Who lives, who does not?
Who pulls the plug on the vegetable?
When does quality turn to quantity?
What is unreal, what is tangible?

Who controls this oxygen machine
Doctor,nurse, or assistant hit me
set the drug in these veins for comfort
I cannot see thee.

Sparrows attempt seduction
on the once empty windowsill
I cannot hear the sirens anymore
only vacant abandon still.

Who eliminates my elimination
the bedpan needs cleaning
getting very angry submerged in shit
the I.V. seems to be leaking.

Pulled the needle
shut the machine off
by my own hand
darkness so soft.

SCOTT ALDERSON

Untitled

Sunday afternoon
marshmallow clouds hover
squirrels' storing nuts
hibernation time soon.

TV vacant
dark screen luminescent
living room complacent
I'm home alone.

Senses tuned to everything
creak of the floorboards;
upstairs neighbours
chow down on my music.

Sunday afternoon
what to do?
when all I crave
all I hunger for
is you.

Fence needs erecting
as do I
but alas I'm lazy
Sunday afternoon hazy.

Untitled

'Twas a brilliant sunny day
when chaos lunged out his fist
to play with yours truly,
together we bashed it out
the victim and the aggressor
mortal combat on the menu.

clouds astonishingly appeared.

we tumbled like children
old chaos and me
till I eliminated him emotionally
and he lay as a wounded soldier
of my misfortunes.

"Be gone old one
I've no time to play
when the sun beckons
to be released from the clouds."

The jet streams swooshes
the clouds disappear
from chaos to carelessness
serenity in a joint.

SCOTT ALDERSON

Glimpse of Heaven

Glimpse of heaven
walked through the door
I shook
trembling as an alien discovered.

I spoke to the vision
more than just a mirage
she spoke
birds sang in my ears telepathically.

psychokinetically
she pulled me in
not knowing
my spirit had awoke anxiously.

Glimpse of heaven
left before I could say farewell
coffee, tea
please.

Existential Moment

Who is he?
that sleeps under dream stars
that walks through castle halls
to find treasures.

Who is she?
that kisses sunbeams on a hardwood floor
that offers me this apple
to become celestial.

Who are they?
to decide the fate of the few
to sell food out of Safeway stores
while peasants perish.

Who am I?
that bears the sword of tongue
that reproduces on paper
to reach enlightenment.

SCOTT ALDERSON

Alien Abduction

Sunday evening, rainy roadway
saw bright light, laser pathway;
lost control of my vehicle
lost control of my bladder
lost consciousness for a moment.

Prodded awake, sharp scalpels
was prodded politely, brain teased;
lost ability to fight
lost control of my bladder
lost consciousness for a moment.

Returned Friday, daring darkness
saw my vehicle, driver's door open;
sprinted gracefully into the seat
jammed the key from pocket to ignition
sped away like a cheetah.

We'll Dance Again

Visualizing the former
what was once day to day
is now but a memory
adolescent in adult garb.
For years we danced the tango
felt love so passion filled
walls crumbled into gravel
and dragons were faced head on.

But forever subsided
present took its toll
now cold winds torment our skin
where there was once warmth
drafts keep us apart.
So I go on with life
facing blizzards alone
with ravens and vampires
circling above the snow.

Two roads are diverging up ahead
will I take the one less travelled?
Or fall back into monotony
comfortability and inner death.
Remember me
I'll remember you always
maybe someday in a different dimension
we'll dance the tango again.

SCOTT ALDERSON

Late Night Television

3:00 a.m.
the masters of marketing
sell sleaze on the screen.

Channel whatever
1-900 number flashing
where an English subtitle
fits in a French pornographic movie.

Today's top 40 dance music as background
red and blue lights
on a smoky dance floor.
Shawna introduces herself
states her womanly needs
call now, don't delay
rescue this lovely damsel
from another lonely night.

$2.99 a minute
must be over 18
adults only, call now
discretion assured
redemption secured
don't delay
time to pay
will be much later
looking for love are you?
masturbator.

Emotional Suicide to Joyous Bliss

Darkness so soft
peace easily achieved
no more payments to the piper
who should have been slaughtered.

A razor blade
brought me here
from sunlight to this
darkness so soft
but, it's all illusion.

The darkness betrays
peace is the myth;
damn the razor blade
for giving me a way out.

I seek the light
crawling on sore knees
bandaging my wrists
with toilet paper
to greet the masses.

I've returned happy
from darkness so soft
think I even found joy
bliss this poet's bounty,
"Shall we dance the tango?"

SCOTT ALDERSON

Supernatural Seduction

Supernatural seduction
black cat crosses your path
dancing on a white fence;
you walk
under the ladder
believing in higher powers
only when in question
of your own mortality.

In an airplane crash
will you survive?

Did you glance at the tarot cards
or kiss the rabbit's foot?

Pray before impact
seek belief
if only for a second.

Dew

Morning awakening
birds seduce me
with their rhapsody.

Squirrels dance
upon blades of grass
new day is born
new dawn caresses naked feet.

Morning dew
squishes between toes
"How long has it been?"
since we worshipped sunrise
and felt content in today.

Come, come dance the daisies
in the field of your dreams
rejoice for life is here, today
grasp it with weathered hands
feel the beauty of warmth
even through the extreme cold.

SCOTT ALDERSON

We Play

We play this silence tag
you're it, I'm it
eyes work their magic
together we could fit.

We play this game
for morality's sake
must keep the primitive
locked up and chained.

We exchange glances
on the sly peripheral
a reflection in my eyeglasses
must confront this visual.

We play with tinker toy
matchbox cars and hot wheels
to entertain our energies
to escape from what is real.

Bee

She occupies the bench
as a candle unlit
conversing in foreign dialect
to the worker bee beside her.

Together debating
the fate of the hive
but time is their enemy
it is I who must thrive.

With a magnifying glass
I perform this senseless act
burning them with sunlight
till they melt into the bench.

SCOTT ALDERSON

Grey Matter Caged in my Head

The kites of knowledge
does not hover over
the grey matter caged in my head.

The late Shakespeare
whom we are forced to study
in arenas of education,
mocks me from his grave site.
How stupid I havebeen
were the future somehow foreseen,
I would not be bankrupt.

"Let loose the kite kind sir,
these are not the feet of swine
only misguided masters
trying to cut the puppet strings
to achieve freedom."

The wind promises hope
re-energizing
the grey matter caged inside my head.

The late Freud
whom we consider a founder
of techniques to study
the grey matter caged in my head
applauds me from his grave site.
How brilliant I've been
To take pleasure as a goal
to remain anonymous in a crowded room.

Words are Power

Words are power
gentle or strong
inspiring or damaging.

Cite the Bible
symbol of all that is Christian
merely words on paper
divine or not is not the issue
yet people are killed
on the basis of their beliefs,
innermost instincts shunned
to destroy the Arab sheik.

Words are power
just ask Rushdie
in exile underground
like the gopher he burrows.
The Koran but a book
holy or flowery makes no difference
for fundamentalist fever to provoke fear
needs only a bullseye to focus on.

Does the atheist quiver
at the mention of God's divine name??
Probably not, but he'll pray
moments before death steals his essence.

Belief in nothing
is still belief
but leaves a void
for poison to permeate
believe in the words that fill you
set dreams free to imagine
something much, much better for this world
John Lennon lyrics come to mind
"Imagine there's no…"

SCOTT ALDERSON

Playboy Photographer

View my lens
see the depth
focus, set shutter speed
expose not film but flesh
beauty accompanied by silk
lace and nylons
fantasies in the flash.

Strap my third eye on
feel it for size
can you see beyond the nakedness
to release the spirit?

They will pay me well
to set the scene
eroticism or pornography
who decides what's obscene?

View my lens
see slaves of beauty
adorning themselves
for big bucks and glamour
fame and glory from nudity
perfume and garter belts
make the print a centrefold,
I'm the photographer.

Jaywalk

Having problems conforming
social control stressing me out
Vitamin B non-effective
tornado of rebellion in the forecast
no doubt.

Kicking over postal boxes
big resentment against Canada Post
checking out the working girls on the corner
deciding which wench I'd like to mate with
the most.

Daydreaming revolution
jaywalking just to spite the enforcers
Glock pistol holstered thus confined
ticket issued to yours truly
for not obeying traffic signals
for not walking within the lines.

Thrown in remand centre
for outstanding fines
for outstanding in the middle of the street
for having independent thoughts
now I'm doing time.

SCOTT ALDERSON

Showed civil disobedience
by jaywalking during lunchtime rush
although there were no cars coming
cops considered chaos unappealing
now I sit in judgement
while the jury lies bleeding
transfusion for the rebel.

Faith in Forever

Copyright 1998

Scott Alderson

Introduction

Well reader here it is book number four already. A style has been formed, an attitude reflected. Three Small White Mice Travelling at the Speed of Light was my first volume of poetry and attracted a wide readership. It was raw and unrefined. Naked in his Rotted Cage came in 1995 and brought a change with it. 1996 and Reflective Energies brought forth yet another stylistic alteration. I really hope you enjoy Faith in Forever as much as I enjoyed putting it together. Special thanks to Rein Vanderkuil for all his assistance in the production end of things. Hope to see you at a reading sometime, reader, and until next time, adieu.

Your often humble narrator,

Scott Alderson

Know

Know the dark side
of someone so close
you'd call significant
no matter how sweet the solitude
of seeing them
as merely radiant

know the secrets
of a forgotten past
you'd know the person
no matter how deep the current
necessary to navigate
so as to expose truth

know passion
for it knows you
prancing around naked
thinking no one was looking

know the sane side
of someone so close
you'd call significant
no matter how bizarre the insanity
of being addicted
maybe even complacent

know the person
know the self.

When

When Tiananmen Square was a bloodbath
sponsored by authority
He shook his head

When Roman soldiers
put a carpenter to wood
He shook his fist

When he used to sell pepper spray to prostitutes
till the cops shut him down,
He at least knew he had protected someone's daughter

one of his former customers appeared in today's obituaries
and he cried in defeat.

Did Anyone Care ?

So sad, she said
so sad indeed
that we share so much
yet so little
that we love so much
yet so little
that at any given time
we could call it quits
and would anyone really care?

Some may rejoice, I proclaim
some may rejoice indeed
that we have so little in common
yet share so much need
that we live in different worlds
dwell in different cellars
hide in different caves
have different fears
yet I know you so well

Many viewed the misery
when at last they dissolved
fraction of a foot away
inches within touch
yes indeed they observed
they cared
even enough just to say,
"I'm sorry it didn't work out"
they're sorry

SCOTT ALDERSON

I'm sorry
you're sorry
but did we really care?

Colony

Within a colony they existed
sheltered from worldly influence
with the righteousness of belief
and the dignity of hard work
to guide them through this life
today they grace the media place
front page newspaper headline
charged by the system enforcers
with crimes against man and the God
to which they profess belief in.

Outside the colony they were mocked
even at the farmers market to which they flocked
people said they were inbred

Incest
sexual assault
victimization no matter what label is attached to it.

Who the hell do they think they are?
I thought I knew who they were.
They always seemed so identifiable
their clothing, their look
even remembered studying colonies in public school
in some social studies book
but these are not they to which I read about
these are just another batch of misguided souls.

Dominatrix

She had been a prostitute for nearly 20 years
said she could make men shake
by using her tools
her whip
her thigh-high boots
most of all
her pornographic language
she spewed from her foul mouth

She dressed like a prostitute
but looked like a victim
a sexually-abused actress
performing for her clientele
to secure her daily bread

She medicated to face life
self-prescribed slave to cocaine
believing that somehow
it would take away her pain
in the end,
it cost her, her life.

Remembered in a memory
of someone once known
dressed up dominatrix
sexual abuse victim clone
sleep well.

SCOTT ALDERSON

Gender War

Caught cowering in combat fatigues
desperately needing a wash
entrenched in a gender war
communication elimination
siege of silence

Skills obsolete
so busy defending
cannot find common ground
on which to meet

So the cycle continues
like a dryer in need of repair
tumbling with no heat
only cold shoulders on which to cry

Maybe men are from mars
who's to say?
Time to gain more understanding
so everything will be okay.

Magnetic

Your eyes could liquify the coldest
male heart
leaving stunned, dazed beyond reality
absorbing more than any paper towel ever made.

We met where again?

53 street you say
funny, what was it we discussed?
Oh yeah, why I am a poet and not involved instead
in a moneymaking enterprise
the sex or drug trade maybe.

Choices I guess.

Magnetized by green eyes
standing in a pool of water
melted heart.

SCOTT ALDERSON

Together in the Head

Summers day lacking clouds
red dress on a park bench close to downtown,
gorgeous female with crossed legs
letting silent breeze caress her genitals

cars humming by like a roller coaster symphony
admirer catches at a glance of erect nipple
catches a memory in his mind
drifts silently into fantasy

together in the head
wanting each other
for that moment more than any other before.

Eyes energizing one another they embraced
leaking liquid escaped down the leg
uncontrollable passion released
they found themselves pacing love
to God's music.

Sirens in the distance
found our couple back in the present
back on a park bench close to downtown
admirer and recipient exchange good byes
disappointment clouds blue sky

later
early evening

fantasy becomes reality
under sweat-drenched sheets.

Prey

Difficult to respond
when a threat is spit
into invisible air
suddenly full of anxiety

politeness floats away
tiger attacks its prey
psychological warfare
results in destruction
as it was spawned
from an alcoholic example
placed in childhood

will an apology suffice?
with intense damage done
tried all my life to be nice
tried hard to sing a happy song
yet here lay I, exhausted
prey bleeding at my side.

Memory

Young love bred alongside music memories
ripens as the interlude is intercepted
by adult words such as betrayal
leaves an impact to last a lifetime

so fragile, young hearts
so deep stems emotion
so cruel, the fall
such empty withdrawal
so intense, but for a while

Adult love bred alongside music memories
continues to expand
beyond shadow of a doubt
with words such as content
this is what they meant
leaving impact to last a lifetime.

Secret

Whispers down a hallway
"psst, psst, can I tell you a secret?"

deal went down quickly behind closed doors
secret meeting in secret chamber
interrogation for information begins
bearer of the secret tells all;

"you must first know what a secret is,
in silence they exist, invisible winds they travel
shaping a pretentious reality, some have suggested
they make us sick
these secrets we choose to keep
like fungi they grow, as grass we fertilize them
till they are spread as a suicide jumper
with someone else scraping up the remains.
Secrets may harm us, may save us
for now may they comfort us
another imperfection in an imperfect world.
Simply put,
touch soul, interrogate mind
unlock chamber, secrets fly."

Whispers down a hallway
"psst, psst, want to hear another secret?"

second deal unclothed itself faster than the first

SCOTT ALDERSON

"In comprehending the first and staying for the second,
the gap has been sewn, from ignorance to understanding
ease comes now, peace of conscience returned
they won't harm us now
these secrets we choose to keep
simply put
I love you.

The Spark

When at last they achieve
their eyes cannot deceive
the spark
spark of passion
sign of love's release.

All are awed
all are envious
energy not contained
makes one nearly delirious.

Like an uncontained virus
spreading via touch
the spark of desire
it's meant for all of us.

Some believe they can catch it
like the common cold
by sharing saliva
striving
as an animal attempts to thrive
setting traps filled with bait.

The task becomes delayed gratification
within another's arms no satisfaction
the spark
spark of passion

Faith in Forever   dies with love's annihilation.

Stay together
let not the spark wither
wear it in the eyes
this crown, your majesty deserves.

Freedom to Be

Wonder if you'll be there
when at last I descend from righteousness
to land on the rocks below
broken bones
immobile
pain all I feel
no Kodak moments left
no spasm of muscles
normally attended to

wonder if you'll be there
open heart, open hands
to receive the promised gift
freedom to be
at last together
you and me
no hurdles to pass
no façades, no masks
freedom to be

wonder if you'll be there
when at last we ascend to equality
to grow closer to one
mobile
joy, ours to feel
happiness for real
normally unattainable

SCOTT ALDERSON

Lair

"I'll love you more than anyone ever has before,"
she pronounced then motioned to another room
"let me show you my talents"
she choreographed as she had many times previous

late evening thunderstorm
brought an instance of lightning
as if God was to intervene
shaking the house
as if to say "Beware"

"lay down with me"
plush pillows cushioned her hair
"dance naked on this bed with me"
she requested entry into my lair

late evening thunderstorm
cast a second coat of lightning
heard the sound once more
of God's disapproval
shaking the house
as if to say "Beware"

"I can't explain why but I must go"
left her exposed with wet inner thighs
"sealed my fate elsewhere, this is not the place to be
for a man identical to the one in the mirror
for a man who has integrity."
The sky suddenly cleared.

Not the First Time

Will is hearing voices again
believes someone is calling his name
over a two-way radio

certainly not the first time
probably not the last time
his sanity lies in question.

in a former life he was a Christian
battling gladiators, playing with lions
in the big coliseum

slaughtered by the Romans
altered his path forever
to return Schizophrenic

Will is hearing voices again
this one says he's God
this one is telling him
to end his existence.

SCOTT ALDERSON

Skinhead

Why'd you shave your head?
did you tire of paying high auto insurance
because others talk on the cell phone while driving
and this is your show of defiance

Why'd you shave your head?
seems you are everywhere
working in convenience stores
$5.00 an hour
to scare victims of the holocaust
that's real white power

why then, why?
for decades we fought your look
bought wigs, treatments, the whole book
yet here you are

bizarre
can't tell the bigots
the intolerant,
from the trendy.

Why'd you shave your head
you wear no swastika on your lapel
you damn not non-Aryans to hell
you appear irrational

Assault

Witnessed physical assault two days back
maybe saved a man's life,
who knows what may have happened
had the battle been allowed to continue

seems many are over the edge
of perverse sanity
drawn deeply into darkness
snapped as a fragile twig
taking on the world
one assault at a time

pulled my van over, honked the horn
issued warning to assailant
of my witness to the crime he was committing
he subsequently disengaged
retreated from his attack
I returned to work mode.

Experiment in Eden

Stepped over an anthill
attempted to enter Eden
pushed door
should have pulled it,
even so,
twas out of service
elevator also condemned
rat infested entranceway
small teeth nibbling on exposed toes.

Kicked in Eden's entrance
destroying former door
was greeted by men in suits
women in uniforms
stockings or pantyhose
garter belts, corsets, who knows?

downtown decadence
speed zone, no decline
rush, rush, rush
heart attack city, pay no mind

delivered destiny
into Eden's courier desk
porters paid the price of courtesy
tripped bomb before it could be diffused
explosion ensued within moments
wounds could not be soothed
yet walls remained
foundation intact
everything similar to normal in fact
seems explosion was implosion
blood vessel blew in my brain.

SCOTT ALDERSON

State of Disunion

Detach and desensitize
plague of violence on TV
like plague growing on a tooth
rotting roots in a mouth

television babysat the last generation for too long
now they reflect it in today's songs
of pain and suffering they've been exposed to
detached and desensitized
got scared and formed a gang

street gang in formation
lacking information
on a better way to be
could they only see
Utopia
they would probably stare in disbelief.

state of disease
state of disorder
state of mind
state of being
state ununited
state of disunion

proud, strong, and free
detached and desensitized
to what they call entertainment
on the big TV screen.

O say you can see
I can and did.

Who Are They ?

They perform here
their roles as producers
pods with peas
working class poor folk.

They have to work
it is not choice
it is necessity
are you going to pay their rent?

lacking smiles most often times,
reality-based organism are you happy?

thought not
for the lens looked through
shows a slide
one cannot deny
many lack in contentment
more often contempt
angry festering fits of frustration.

Maybe
if they found passion
reason to smile
thing to activate motion from bed in morning
movement without warning.

SCOTT ALDERSON

Shallow

That lifestyle attached to your being
is too packed with shit
as if constipated somehow
cracked, packed, and painful
leaves you looking so very shallow.

That lifestyle so boldly chosen
of hiding in shadows
carefully unexposed to light
dark, dank and smelly
leaves you black not white.

Everybody else's time is precious not mine
yet riddle me with guilt all the time
but I finished answering
my machine finally died.

Now cold
standing in the shadows alone
left vacant
without quarter for phone.

Shiver here
shiver there
a lifestyle full of shit
is definitely to be feared.

Lifestyle oh lifestyle
what a mess yours is
but the problems no longer excite me
now they're yours and his.

Home Invasion Robbery

Watching a movie
maybe real life
acting out a role
husband and wife

raising several offspring
in winter, summer, and fall
dazzled by responsibilities
working overtime to feed them all

woke from deep sleep one night
strange sound in silent house
tiptoe, tiptoe
could it be a mouse?

young offenders offending
broke in through locked door
three juveniles who should have been asleep
threw a family of five upon a floor

dramatizing a dramatization
placed the gun into a mouth
pulled a trigger, then ran
last known headed South.

SCOTT ALDERSON

Instant Coffee In A Cup

Sitting at a kitchen table
instant coffee in a cup
smoking
thinking
listening to birds chirping
uncaged
well fed
wonder what they are saying

excreting words from brain to paper
woke up from one of those dreams
so real to life
so sharp to cut
so sad it was not true.

Debated going back to the strange bed
back to the strange dream state
emotional health will not permit this
trying too hard to repair damage, not encourage more

overwhelmed at a kitchen table
instant coffee in a cup
crying
hysterical
lost in a different time
uncaged
well-fed
wonder what I'm saying.

Once

Once spotted a singer
upon stage trimmed with Christmas lights
quartz halogens suspended from a ceiling
got all excited inside
butterfly warm fuzzy feeling

seduced by potential masses
dreamed a dream of fame and fortune
sold it to preserve sanity
to face reality
realized dream did not die
nor did the dreamer
he just aged a little more
little more gracefully at that.

Once spotted a singer
singing a different tune than before
teaching through the naked word
in favour of his melodies being heard
sang and danced better than the pro
received standing ovation
little did he know
he cracked somewhere down the line.

Navigating

Souls sailing
winds of change caressing
navigating channel of crisis
enduring eye of storm
to reap rewards.

Standing erect
two bodies side by side
facing opposition
facing distraction
vulnerable vessels of flesh.

Lack of time
enemy that taunts believers
non-friend of lovers
impending necessity
drives minutes into seconds

Disillusioned grey matter from two minds
redevelops hope to carry on
composing
continually
striving
to be free to feel.

Microbe

Eye on a microscope
manipulating magnification
to clarify
viewed glass slide,
hand prodding with tweezers
gentle exploration
to observe specimen response

movement on a glass slide
hands reaching for a camera
Kodak moment on a microscope
fingers press activate
all is recorded.

SCOTT ALDERSON

Integrity

Who sells themselves anyway, any day
to secure some cash? compromising integrity
to found their personal stash.
We're all prostitutes one way or another
while some get paid more
others merely survive.

Who turns their back on personal integrity
pays dearly in the end
conscience is a nasty enemy
underestimated and cunning.

We're all prostitutes, who's your pimp?
seven sins to choose from
what line does your integrity cross?

Faith in Forever

Lacking an ability
to sketch upon this page
words to describe emotions experienced
the past year today we recall

images imprinted of brilliance
radical facial expressions so significant
power of bonding so understated
misunderstood by most

Still lacking an ability
to convey or converse
the crevices of a wounded heart
repaired not to be ever again torn apart

moments lasting hours
affection activating power
of need, of passion
internal/external chemical reaction

lay with me
lie unto me
tell me
this is faith in forever.

SCOTT ALDERSON

Faith in Forever

If we woke up tomorrow
and the world had dissolved
it would not mean the end of us
nor the death of our love

If we ran to others
to fix upon the needle
the injury might be too deep
cost of gratification too steep

lay with me
lie unto me
tell me
this is faith in forever.

Till whatever makes us part
if God's will it from the start
of all the treasures you've bestowed
faith in forever
is the debt to you I owe.

Acknowledgements

I wish to acknowledge all the lovers that have seen me through a volume of poetry in production. The patience and understanding they demonstrated was very commendable. I also wish to acknowledge all the new and used bookstores that have stocked Scott Alderson Poetry on their shelves. Thank you for your continued support.

In addition I wish to thank West Canadian Industries Ltd. for their assistance in the production end of this project. Lastly, I wish to acknowledge all the children in my life, their innocence and keen observations of this world have helped to title this book. Many thanks again reader, stay tuned for the next volume.

Someone drove my car into a wall, before I could do it: A collection of poems

Dedication

This work is dedicated to the individuals who have shared in my life experience. Thank you. Special thanks to Rein Vanderkuil for his help in the production of this work

Introduction

Book 5 is here. When I began writing, I had a vision of putting a collection of poetry together. I did not foresee the birth of five books. I am pleased. This past year of 1999 has been hard to say the least. Many changes have come upon my life. This book is the legacy I leave. My books are my children… I hope you enjoy them.

Poetry is a passion for me somewhat spawned by music lyrics and totally spawned by life experiences. If you are an aspiring writer, then I say to you believe in yourself and do not fall prey to what others tell you. Other people will tell you stuff like, "You won't be famous until you die," and "Don't quit your day job." For every person who attempts to calm the wave, there will be others who will say to you, "You really moved me with that poem" or "I feel you have talent."

Believe the optimists and go forward.
Shameless self-promotion prevails.
Remember, writing poetry is like making love,
it has to have rhythm.

Scott Alderson

Hive

Like a cold turning to pneumonia
traffic on these roadways
has become congested.

Tiny motorized bumblebees
cruising round the industrial hive
cutting each other off
showing stingers in aggression.

Occasionally killing one another
drinking pollen then flying
intoxicated behind the wings.

In order to make honey
we have to return safely to our hives.

No Good

This telephone does not ring anymore
I wonder if it is defective
passed by inspector 99
should have been rejected

worked fine for years
nightly at nine o'clock
it rang until answered
and your voice seduced me

This telephone does not ring anymore
I wonder if I paid the bill
it is now eleven o'clock
and you have not called still

symbolic of the breakdown
even the phone company cannot commit
to a suitable time they could stop by
to take a look at it

So, I am left with a defective phone
which like an impotent penis
does me no good.

SCOTT ALDERSON

Climax

"There," she cried out loud
"there, that's the spot, ummm"
eyes closed she clenched the sheets tighter.
"I am pleased to see you smile," he responded
together in daylight
curtains wide.

For hours they danced on the waterbed
without feeling nausea.

"Hold me close to your chest, for I surely believe
it is the place I like best." she said soothingly

"Sweat pearls are running rampant on my forehead
and thus you will be soaked, access denied."
he rolled over and went to sleep.

Sometimes the climax is not the height of the story.

Love is Not a Curse

What's up?
What's going down?
All this talk from new age prophets about how
love can be.
I've been talking and walking for years
worshipped and feared it in the same thought
even tenderized my heart
I still believe in love.

After all the abuse
after all the shit was flushed
only I remained

New age, old age
new testament, old testament
road more of less chosen
genders from different planets
in the now time
every time
choose love
is the theme over and over.

work it baby
feel it
let passion be your host
derive from love the most
intense feelings for better, for worse
love is not a curse.

Selfish Nature

Observe the demise of family
retirement homes full of parents
we had to abandon, so our three jobs could be done
all this time exhausted
chasing the elusive key to success

success is being alive
each day, each breath,
seldom do we wake
and recall this simple truth.

Observe the increase in relationship breakdown
why at any given moment
I can ponder at least three couples
in danger of divorce
for better, for worse
all the time exhausted
working three jobs to keep the mortgage.

Observe the selfish nature of human
then maybe we can stop replacing
parents with puppies
and show concern for children.

Government should not have to force a person
to take responsibility for their kids or their
parents.

Set the World on Fire

Sick of diseases killing masses
tired of homeless within the classes
sick and tired
fed up and uninspired
time to light the fuse
a torch to make my muse
let's set the world on fire

frustrated by inconsiderate bastards,
wishing God would return faster
frustrated and wishing
while the politicians go fishing
hope they fall overboard
without them we can afford
to set the world ablaze

disappointed by the status quo
no longer wanting to buy the world a cola
disappointed and no longer hoping
agitated by just merely coping
time to light the fuse
a torch to make my muse
time to set the world on fire.

Burn fuckers burn, may God have no mercy
fire and brimstone, vacant and alone
time for the meek to enjoy the feast
upon oppressive overlords

SCOTT ALDERSON

Pretty Much Daily

Pretty much daily,
postman delivers bills
to an un-enchanted recipient.
Agoraphobic individual
scared of the outside world waits
until postman visits neighbours
before unlocking the deadbolt
to retrieve their bills from the black box.

A night on the town could result in an extended
stay in a psychiatric ward
if only there was an empty bed
in a local hospital
not suffering government cutbacks.

Pretty much daily,
doctor delivers babies
to the un-enchanted world.
Completely helpless individual
lacking life through breath
waits for doctor to slap their ass
before screaming and crying
to say, "Hello, here I am."

Confusion

This dispute
is not about another woman
or another man
it is about us.

It is about commitment
a coupled future
to coincide with a coupled past.
Readiness appears lacking
I am ready to catch the train
you are still buying your ticket.

Transmission

Lost drive
shifted into neutral
by a set of circumstances
a series of events
a multitude of nuances.

could not back up
reverse rapidly receded
another symptom of the damaged road
another direction not heeded

Sitting in neutral on a hill
lost power, lost will
to drive, to move
cannot talk, cannot cruise
this time I blew the tranny.

Airport

Many ways to define beauty
one is;

the quality of being very pleasing
in form, colour, tone, etc.

although this describes you
it is still lacking
for you are a beauty undefined
a priceless diamond shining and refined
yours is that which transcends physical limitations
yours is that which took change for its arrival
and as a life of pain departed
the Airport was reopened
allowing travellers to see your beauty
for perhaps the first time.
I am pleased to land at your Airport.

SCOTT ALDERSON

Seasonal Affective Disorder

Took a long time
for winter to arrive
dressed to kill
coldest bitch created
virginal in appearance
lethal by injection
hypothermic happiness here I come.
January finds me empty
loss of love took away inspiration
light is limited as darkness rules the season
compounding my negative frame of mind.

How long is the wait for spring?
I dream warmth and am somehow soothed
I welcome opportunity and romance
who will draw my bath?
who will feed my pet?
when I cease to exist
what season will it be?

Upbringing

Dad died at an early age
early for him, early for me
I was but an infant of 22 months old
Dad was 45.

Lacking life insurance
Mother lacking an education
the welfare cycle began
in the welfare capitalist country
to which I was thrown into by birthright.
Shame ensued shortly thereafter
we could not keep up with the Jones's
in fact, we did not even know who they were.
Imagination replaced monetary wealth
maybe as religion does for worshippers.

Alcoholism moved into my home
during the impressionable years
the subsequent emotional breakdown
was a bit of foreshadowing.
Adolescence advanced towards me
puberty and ridicule went hand in hand
till drugs were introduced.
Dad died young
will I?

SCOTT ALDERSON

Stiffness

Foam bubble bath on an ass cheek
evaporates
when a towel is applied,
only to be replaced
by the moisture of my lips upon it.

Erotic you say,
reality if I may.

Ten years from now
I'll still kiss your ass
without being asked to do so
what is even more bizarre
is that I am going to like it.

Foam bubble bath on a nipple
evaporates
when blown on
and leaves only a stiffness in its wake.

Wrote This in Under 10 Minutes

Would have escorted you through eternities
entrance
provided you could have kept silent and discreet
upon being welcomed by the gate master.
Would have combed your hair for days
had it been required, even desired.
Should have held you in my arms
till death did we part.
Summer's heat drives me horny
winter's cold makes me shiver alone
stress develops from hours spent
patiently waiting by the telephone.
Would have massaged you head to toe
all you had to do was appreciate me
but it seems the task was too much for you
our loss I guess.

SCOTT ALDERSON

Another Way of Saying I Love You

Rather than having us write music
created by our souls
with a pencil
only to reap anguish when it is erased,
we could write it with this pen.

Rather than dealing with longing
never desired a woman so much,
we could covet compromise
to try better understanding
to reach a peaceful solution.

Rather than being lonely and alone
let's be together.

Rather than thinking about differences
let's focus on similarities
peculiarities and all that stuff
all the delicacies at love's table
await for us to feast on.

Rather than doing anything else for a day
I'd like to kiss the back of your knees
your legs, your buttocks
before I bore weight on your pelvis
slowly entering you from behind.

Inner Forest Fire

Going in for inspiration
seeking something in a magazine
message of importance
delivered by a headline caption
take a topic
vindicate a value
slide a slant
to a controversial subject matter
then kick an apathetic nation
in its ass.

The forest is burning
but who the fuck cares
tree upon tree lost
in a non-English speaking country
where young girls are sold into the sex trade
for drugs her father needs,
forgive the father for he has sinned,
I don't think so.

SCOTT ALDERSON

Ride the Wave

Liquidated all assets
pawned plenty piles of crap
through it all they laughed
mockingly said, "He's come undone"
still he continued
rejecting all they had foreshadowed
everything they had set out for him
and the way life should be.
He had not chosen his addiction
It chose him so he thought
smoking crack cocaine by the ticking of the clock
tic toc tic toc so he thought
as sanity slowly slipped through his palms
a dead like calm overshadowed
his bachelor apartment
they said he had overdosed.

This One Is For Nobody

This one is for tobacco companies
trying to get your kids addicted
and the crack dealer
killing the innocence of childhood

this one is for VLTs
it is for monopolies
not for RISK

Parker Brothers invented the games
the Capitalist plays them everyday
as he kicks the squeegee window washer kids
off of the corner because the skinhead
represents some revolution
that seeks to shake his world

This sounds like a headstones ballad
all geared up and politically padded
but this is just about the absurd.

SCOTT ALDERSON

Friday

Sought to vacate apartment
nurtured thoughts of dance bar
time to go fishing
tired of mere wishing
life would knock at my door.

Scored a taxi
scored some dope
random acts of entertainment
felt inclined to float;
bound to the ground.

Tiptoed lightly past the cabbies fair
to dance divinely should I choose to dare
perchance we met upon the floor
two eagles who chose to soar.

enough fantasy
such blatant audacity
reality is a couch alone
inside rented apartment
toilet for a throne
it is Friday night.

Altruism

Risking vulnerability
perchance to dare
compassion and concern
what is the cost to care?

Was the price too high
when the beggar died
to give him proper burial.

was it Christmas time
or the fourth of July
when in somber moment
you looked around
began to cry.

not martyr
nor saint
upon this cold landscape
could paint
a warm fuzzy moment

who cares?
perchance to dare
in an altruistic headspace
how would you fair?

SCOTT ALDERSON

No Patience

Patience flew out the window
at a time when its usage was not complete
pinched at air to try to retrieve it
unsuccessful at the attempt

once gone never to return
with similar magnitude
thus we must create
must provoke artificial patience

did time ever decelerate
even long enough to retrieve breath?

reservoir nearly drained
precious resource
once wild, now tame
need more time

artificial not sufficient
lack of control causing distress
need to be normal
can't keep fantasy forever

did time ever decelerate
even long enough to retrieve breath?

What Wretchedness

What wretchedness hath besieged
the human collective sealing its demise
from altruistic warmth
to cold falsity of belief based on lies.

In the early years of Anno Domini
man named Jesus Christ did decree
love your neighbour
love your fellow human;
love turned to hate
for the monsters we chose to create
cannot be stopped
now or evermore.

Seven sins to indulge in
indeed we've tried them all
then paused briefly
tried to prevent our fall
from a ledge of grace
a perch perhaps
moment of truth upon us
had placed into lap.

Is it too late for change?

Can altruism once again prevail?
upon the sea of truth shall we set sail?

Tired of clinging to outside of lifeboat
time to climb inside joining human family
to unseal our demise.

SCOTT ALDERSON

Artificial Heat

Inside artificial heat
two hands on one wheel
two feet on one pedal at a time
synchronicity in motion
following concrete crayon marks
four wheels in one lane
radio reminiscing
karaoke driver.

He remembers date, time, maybe place
mesmerized by a memory
unfocused on task at hand
mentally envisioning a promised land
he imagines a writer interned
overseas prison
yes indeed he is concerned
for one who shares his passion.

Inside artificial heat
two hands on one wheel
two feet on one pedal at a time
synchronicity in motion.

Short Week

Thursday
tempting taste buds
suggest nourishment
on an outdoor patio
brunette waitress
tray loaded with beer
shirtless
sunny soon
clouds temporary
minor disruption
for an alcoholic intention
drawn to consume.

Friday
finally frazzled
end of a busy week
relaxation on tomorrow's menu
think I'll pamper myself
brainless
suntanning silently
cops shot the neighbour
because he was dealing crack.

Hood

Sprawled out spread eagle-like
on the hood of a Corvette
damaged, mangled slightly, semi-conscious
got an aching in my head.

Once had a dream of mountain biking
on trails without concrete base
humid summers day creating sweat
water bottle best friend
then awoke on hood of car
here lay I
bruised and disoriented.

Arrival

Awaiting your arrival
will you show?
Every bit of mental energy
focused on sending a message
did you receive it?

How will you answer?
will my doorbell ring
and when I open my front door
will you be at the back
or can this fantasy become today's reality
some kind of love attack.

Passion does not follow the time clock at work
and cannot be subsided by mere thought
so why resist the temptation
to appreciate one another?

I still await your arrival
during probably the longest minute
today has dished out.
The longest hour in today
may through the odyssey illuminate the way
the path, the road we need to take.

Instead of awaiting your arrival
I might have witnessed your departure.

SCOTT ALDERSON

A collection of poems

> The airport is crowded today but my baggage is
> light, maybe I'll have to book another flight.
> Upon this hour's end, there will be no invitations
> nor flowers I forgot to send
> there will be only tears.

SCOTT ALDERSON

Full Beer

The only full beer
in a case of empty bottles
is finally cracked
designed to sound off
when the cap is twisted
left or right
An alcoholic thirst
is never quenched
by mere ingestion.

The last ounce
from a 40-ounce bottle
slides down a throat
designed to numb
already dead senses
deadly disease decaying
from the inside and out.
An alcoholic thirst
is never quenched
till death drink and the drinker part.

Refill the case with hope
and the ability to dream again
maybe for the first time recognize
that indeed shit does and always will be there
to smell up your life.

Scott Alderson

Background

It was misplaced a long time ago
placed on a cupboard and abandoned
black background on white canvas
heart of one who has been divorced.

From the cold winter storm they came
determined to retrieve and revive
black background on a new canvas
heart unthawed pumping blood again.

It was found a short time ago
the ability to feel significant
black background did not cling to canvas
gave up co-dependency to avoid cardiac arrest.

"Artists, choose your background carefully."

Show Courage

I can live without anyone, however,
I cease to thrive without you.
Show courage
be with me forever,
as long or short a time that may be.
Fear not magnificent woman
everyone is timid about becoming vulnerable
I as well, am apprehensive
but your love gives me courage
I am not merely lonely without you,
I cease to be.

I can live without anyone, however,
I cease to thrive without you.
What I want is you
no doubt in my mind
you are the reward at the end of the tunnel
I have heard so much about,
the rainbow after a thunderstorm
the washer that fits inside my water spout.
You are the dream I dreamed
the vehicle I wish to be driven to heaven in
take me there please.
I do not need, I want.

SCOTT ALDERSON

Upon Friendship

When I think upon friendship
I think of you and I
all the struggles and achievements
sent to confront us in this life.
Though the passage of time
has begun to show upon our faces
and it becomes harder to remember
the visits to different places,
one thing I remember is you were there
through it all.
When I think about what constitutes a friend,
loyalty, honesty, integrity, mutual respect, and
acceptance,
I think of you and me.

When the passage of time
erodes this paper to dust
one thing to remember always
one thing to remember you must,
I love you.

Janice

It was never wrong to love you so much
seemed so natural to be welcomed by your touch
none more seductive will ever be found.
It was never wrong to be with you
time treasured till eternity,
turns this page to dust.
Somehow, my soul will find you
when I cease to exist in physical form
and wake from the sleep to which I go.

Someday, in a world without fear
in a world without allergies
I'll be with you again.

It is never wrong to dream about forever
the unpredictability of life prohibits guarantees
but this much is true
I will and always have loved you.
Until tomorrow, adieu.

Bitter Waters

Mouth waters for a taste of wealth
glory, fame
all the riches that eliminate
artistic suffering.

Want to ride in a limousine
luxurious pampering is deserved
want to fly in a plane
got my ticket reserved
travel for lunch
to taste the good life
have I won the lottery yet?
or been given the tax-free grant?

Eye waters for a glimpse of reality
for a welfare recipient
in a welfare state
in a welfare-sanctioned rooming house
owned by slum lords.

The fact that we have ghetto conditions
in such a modern country sickens me.

Implosion

Filled it full of explosives
after removing windows, wiring, and witnesses
then imploded it just to prove a point
but no one understood the point
did not even know who they were
or what they stood for.
Modernization they claimed
hospital to playground they explained
proposed redevelopment on a toxic site
where children play by day
and married men searching for anonymous sex
meet at night in outdoor washrooms.

Still no one understood
the decline of civilization began so fast
explosion, implosion
everything collapsed
and they cleared away the rubble
for reconstruction to begin.
I stood in awe.

SCOTT ALDERSON

Dis Ease

This disease has no cure
that disease has no cure
all current technicians are busy
bogged down with other projects.

This state of dis ease has a cure
that state of dis ease will never be cured
all current energy is busy
bogged down in reality.

Time to dream for awhile
wake me not
rest this vehicle of flesh
this walking mineral.

Fell into the basement of love's condominium
to be revived six weeks later
stumbled up the stairs
to rediscover passion
without anyone's help.

Reconfirmed every thought
I held this truth
that love requires work constantly
that this dis ease has a cure.

Mud Puddle

Drive through pickup window,
change fell from outstretched hand
into large mud puddle never to be seen again.

Corporate policy dictates
all sales are final
no refunds, no exchanges
management not responsible
do you see the irony?

Mud puddle conveniently situated
corporate policy dictated
not responsible for risk
all I want is my change back.

SCOTT ALDERSON

Power Struggle

Set windows down in my Chevy Camaro
cranked stereo to upper volumes
heavy metal guitar licks shout out
to an unconcerned population
long hairs get tangled in the wind
girls on the street admire the driver
vocalizing their approval.

Red light turns to familiar green
like dragsters we accelerate
faster, faster, neck and neck, me and the other guy
blue and red flashes of light behind us
but, the brick wall at the end of the alley
has my name written all over it.

Crack

Scratching carpet with uncut fingernails
searching for pieces of cocaine
jonesin' they call it.
Their quest futile
soon to be "buggin out"
withdrawal warring with brain.

Next day,
argument number who knows
combatants take their mark
ready, set, no blow left
verbal assault becomes physical
insanity's halo
umbrellas furniture less apartment.

Sirens sobbing blocks away
blue and red bodies
lay motionless on carpet
embracing base pipe.

SCOTT ALDERSON

Insecurity

Thunderstorm
wind howling, lightning torches grass
silhouette beckoning with finger appears.

Invited inside sheltered from rain
shared much tea, shared much pain
from which host and visitor benefitted.

Storm surrendered to sunshine and rainbow
together they ran through fields of ceramic
figurines, wondering what tomorrow
would drop upon their persons.

Thunderstorm returned next day
not as severe as was forecast
still serious enough to warrant discussion
the drum of today resounded nature's percussion
as the eagle took flight.
Insecurity turned to infidelity.

For Love or Rhyme

Like music is to ear
poetry is to eye
soothing
angry
emotional.

As painter chooses colours
poet chooses words
carefully constructed consonants
very vocal vowels
to complete his canvas.

For love or rhyme
political outcry or introspection time
poetry soothes the human beast.

SCOTT ALDERSON

Sunday Shopping

For one day only,
could we not just close everything up?
every convenience store
even though it might be inconvenient
the lock on the front door
could be used for a day
not just washroom breaks.

For one day only,
could we cease and desist
what's the problem with it
relax, take a break
death will still be your fate
why not prolong life?

Maybe one day
we will close everything
spend the day with our kids
our families, our companions, ourselves
let us call this day Sunday
oops, somebody already did.

Park to Reverse

Rear view mirror
train passes by
child walking behind vehicle
blind spot
transmission shifting,
park to reverse
just about to release pressure
from foot to brake pedal
caught vision
in objects are closer than they appear mirror
saved a life
spared the child.

SCOTT ALDERSON

Robin

Young robin nests in a mobile home
located beyond central Alberta
her colouring lights the prairie sky
and attracts her mate

he, does not wish to work
male robin will not fly
his wings must have been damaged
by some great thunderstorm

young robins travel together
in Camaro's and Firebirds
down manmade paths
to seek fortune in a new nest

the eagle hovers overhead
robins smile to greet their fate
all will be well.

Goddess

A goddess
compelled to greet the world
with a smile.

Emerald eyes enslave every admirer
entranced they can only mumble.

Fresh from a Victoria's Secret brochure
confident in leather of denim I'm sure,
positive energy belts her waist
leaving many wanting to appreciate
the essence of the cat.

Smile goddess, smile
for yours is a smile
meant to shine forever,
the future is yours.

Cloak of Adulthood

From the hood worn as a child
to a cloak of adulthood
spoken word was relied on
to express emotion

Gullible, I believed you
I believed in us.
I believed them about Santa Claus
Easter bunny, tooth fairy
themes of mystery
themes to spark imagination

Gullible, why is honesty subjective?
held in confidence by honesty's host.

Wonder why the spoken words hurt now.

Reflection at 34

Finally fell from righteousness
surprisingly effortless in the descent
hit bottom again
only to recover stronger
humble and meek.

Will I thus inherit?
Who wants this world?
I merely seek its bounty, love.

did you, do you, love me?
I thought, think so.

I fantasized, idolized, worshipped you
yes indeed,
now here I am bruised but repairable.
Who will be with me next?
I choose to be alone for now at least
time to focus on me.

 SCOTT ALDERSON

Showing Sadness Rarely

Among a group of quitters you were terminated
escorted off the premises, basically humiliated

obscenities escaped your orifice
as you gave the one finger salute
time to find another job
before you are broken and destitute

Among a group of losers
maybe you can win
the bonus prize, the booby prize
win, win, win

horseshoes in your butt
or insurmountable bad luck
how is your life going to be?
one disappointment after another
or will you seize the opportunity?
take a risk, take a chance
stand solid in adversity.

Among a cluster of humans
you can co-exist
showing sadness rarely.

Busy

Travelling frequently between real and ideal
meeting many moody persons on the trip
regardless of their destination
their natural vocation
illustrated by one phrase, "I'm busy"

All the modern conveniences
microwaves and other appliances
were invented to free some time
so we could enjoy our lives
so we could expand our minds,
instead we watch television.

I'm busy
you are busy
they are busy
he is busy
she is busy
the shopping mall
the telephone line
everyone, everything
they are all busy

all the modern crap
makes the pile of shit larger.

SCOTT ALDERSON

As We Gather

As we gather in smoke-filled rooms
lacking proper ventilation.
As we release words into empty air
lacking monetary motivation,
bombs destroy once-lush countryside.

As I bear witness to man's destruction
I retreat to a familiar place where raging wars
find resolution, retreat into my head.

As we gather in non-smoking environments
so impressed with our healthy attitudes,
our tax dollars just blew the hell out of some
stranger's home.
As we release fighter jets into empty air
so impressed with our cruising missiles
the occasional one is bound to hit coffee shops.

As we sit on our buttocks watching war on TV
my hard earned money finds itself
financing mortar shells.

Seeking

Lack of natural light signifies the lapse of time
the process of change
day becomes night.

Upon a cliff as an eagle
I observe
I ponder
I speculate and theorize

To reach the top of the pyramid
to ascend to divinity
what climbing tools do I need?

I don't have enough rope.

SCOTT ALDERSON

Seeking More

I seek a form of love
one that would make God smile
if he was in human form.

Artificial light signifies the manipulation
of an environment
the process of change
dark becomes illuminated.

Upon sleep time
an eagle rests in its nest.

Acknowledgements

The following deserve credit for the inspiration towards this work:

Stephanie E. and Danann E.; Angela K.; Tanya D.; Dr. Kevin Alderson and his children, Troy and Shauna; Kevin Midbo; Janice R. and her children Jesse, Carter, and Amy; Catherine B.;my sponsor and friend Howard C.; my greatest nieces; fellow addicts in recovery; 12 step programs; all the addictions counsellors that have helped me; numerous local writers (Tanya D., Kerry L., Lisa D., Richard B., Christine K., Janet H., Stuart Armour B., William C., and many others); Psalm 83:18; and a special acknowledgement for my mom Hazel.

Thank you all
May Jehovah God look well upon you reader.
Thanks as well to my kindred brothers,
Cam, Rich, Rein, and James.

Another Flush

Dedication

This work is dedicated to my muse.
She knows who she is and if you ever see us
together, you will too.
She is my soulmate.

Introduction

Welcome to another collection of poetry by Scott Alderson. Inside,
you will find a variety of images, expressions, and thoughts that
stimulate a feeling or smile to which you can relate.

Scott began writing in 1983 and began publishing chapbooks and full
size collections in 1994. Countless readings at bookstores and coffee
houses later, Scott has developed a distinctive style within the literary
community.

Born October 15, 1964 in Edmonton, Alberta, Canada to George
Fredrick and Hazel Irene Alderson. He completed high school in Stony
Plain, Alberta and attended Mount Royal College for two semesters in
Calgary. He was kicked out both times, the last resulting in a two-year
suspension. He also tried training as a licensed practical nurse but did
not complete the course. He has worked as a grocery clerk, boat trailer
builder, retail salesperson, security officer, disc jockey, driver, bicycle
courier, dispatcher, direct salesperson, and overall grunt.

Currently, he works full-time as a courier and part-time at a used
bookstore. In between, he writes regularly and attends a writers' group
weekly. In his spare time, he does poetry readings and tries to have a
social life.

Host

Hosted social gathering
Wall-to-wall house party
watched tavern bouncer
kiss and hug a midget in the kitchen

contemplated possible hallucination
questioned current reality
while oil riggers
conducted physical violence on the lawn
and intellectuals quoted Plato in the
master bedroom

Ended bizarre ball
by dancing in my undershorts
under the direction of a full moon
elderly neighbours peeking
through curtained glass
only to decide in finality
decadence was achieved
recognized and perceived
as a treat.

Muse

Before closed eyes at bedtime
images of your nakedness
play precious pandemonium
with inner thoughts

Upon waking with wonder
images of you dressing
infect my psyche
leaving me late for work

Throughout the day
images of you
dance with me.

SCOTT ALDERSON

Untitled

Within a room where no one knows me
anonymous despite my fame

peering into the eyes of strangers
seeking a returning glance
that may lead to ecstasy

several others are scanning this space
prodding and probing the deli counter
flirting with the clerk

I remain bored
anonymously ignored
craving excitement.

Neglect

Recently neglectful
of expressing my delight
upon observing the curves
of your exceptional body

black pants of soft substance
hugging your buttocks,
matching colours of underwear
display themselves on your shoulders

your essence speaks to me
reminding my psyche
of what it is like to dream

SCOTT ALDERSON

September

Snow slinging September
cloud cover chaos
metaphor of my mind

The sky is falling
God weeps at man's imperfections

My faith teeters
my brain totters
I can see
and I saw
madness on the television last night
when does the mind rest?

Dog on Fire

Jack Russell terrier jumping
through a flaming hoop
hairs burned
as the distance was too great

master makes funeral arrangements
secures a plot in pet cemetery
lays down payment on memorial
brass statue of Spunky

what courage he showed
as he jumped the flame
so well-behaved
so well-trained

man's best friend died to amuse his master
to honour him with ribbons.

SCOTT ALDERSON

Memories My Companion

Listening to music we used to call ours
when good times were all we had
before the relationship turned sour
and memories became my companion

Lyrics of love bring tears
to ducts that closed years ago
like a furnace that is just being cleaned
these are wide open now

Scratching at table for tissue
face flooded with emotion
it's clear that I miss you

memories are my companion

goodbye once loved
hello new day.

Tonight inside insomnia
your ghost visits me
I feel angry with you
angry with myself
you lied to me at the airport
looked into my eyes and said,
"I love you"
boarded the plane
and I believed you
guess I got you back though
when I caught you kissing another
and told you that,
"you are the only one, still"

The plane is leaving again
this time you told the truth
about fucking time eh!!!!

SCOTT ALDERSON

Craving the Miracle

Would taking vows before a minister
convince you that my intention
is not sinister

what demons remained to face

cold winds echo the emptiness
that howls internally

craving the miracle
that will reunite

I become impatient

What act of faith is required
demonstrating loyalty
to the one desired?

Does aloneness hurt you as much?
to me, it is death.

Thawed

Ventured upon frozen prairie
watched seasons of warm
come and go
then crossed a mighty glacial crevice
while waiting with patience
for you to join me

Many times you were lost
finding comfort by another's campfire
so I built a shelter
which after several years of illusion,
collapsed
now I am without a home

Once nestled in your passions heat
that thawed the prairie winter
now left to shiver alone
with memories and longings
or years passed

Will you return home once more?

SCOTT ALDERSON

Rain

God's tears continue to meet concrete
as this tormented soul is purged on paper
Will a rainbow complete the sky
when all is written?

why the storm began
is of no consequence
no explanation
for insanity's decadence

necessity lies in solution seeking solemn
moments
and understanding the term,
brainstorm

this man
sculpted in divine image
feels the rain
feels the shame
brought forth from lightning flashes
of dreams dissolved daily

outside this rented shelter
God's tears have ceased
birds once again converse with one
another
while a man in isolation
purges on paper.

Inside

Inside a society of skinheads
Long-haired rebel exists,
offended by the scent of concrete
dampened by summer thunderstorm

stench of city plugs nose
state of confusion plugs head
with nasty thoughts
of unkindness and gloom

inside a city of clones
individual human exists
offended by conformity
brought by business man's rule

stench of fear feels air
state of chaos fills streets
protests and riots
unrest and poverty

inside a mind
switch goes on
assault rifle is cuddled
victim becomes real.

SCOTT ALDERSON

Impaired

What the hell are you thinking?
driving and drinking
alcoholic river in your veins
alcoholic mush in your brain

you could have brought an end to life
for one who had two kids, a home, a wife

could have phoned a cab
bet you wish you had
as an attorney is hailed
asking about your bail
to a judge that thinks you are scum
tolerance level for such behaviour
is none
in the prairie party place

many others drive badly when sober
someone's sister
someone's brother
but you could not care less
impaired driving you take the risk
possible death
alcohol breath
blowing a police person's machine.

You Deserve It

You deserve it
what pleasure to see you smile
this zone entered
lets light lend itself
to your personal energy

after all past hardships
now sailing serenity seaports
to face love again

I admire you,
for a long time courage failed
now I am ready

you deserve it
seize every day

true romance touched soft skin
changing your world
after all chaos ceased
now sailing serenity seaports
to embrace love again

I decide to follow through
take a risk for a long time feared
now I am ready.

SCOTT ALDERSON

Mistake

Oops, sorry
didn't see your colours
your Hells Angels M. C. banner

had I,
probably wouldn't have
punched you when you pushed me

as I sit in this emergency room
I find remorse
and the remaining members
of your chapter here beside me,
keeping me company
genuinely add to this
of course

big mistake
had I thought
even to hesitate
a nose would not be broken
angry words would not be spoken
two warriors would not have met.

War of Understanding Two

Here is my perspective
then there is yours
no mediator in the world
can mend the cuts we cause,
for ours is a limited psyche
maybe better people
more educated, more calm
could converse to conclusion
feelings hardcore deep
showing surface symptoms
sealing our demise.

SCOTT ALDERSON

Flesh

Should have seized the opportunity
when our paths crossed,
to inhale your scent
to brush my hand against
your clothed buttocks.

Should have asked your phone number
should have given you mine
but I fell about lacking courage
didn't seem the right time
to risk rejection
to state my intentions
on worshipping your flesh.

Camping Trip September 96

Walked a pathway
close to a river bank
within mountain park
was thoroughly impressed
pollution hadn't tinged the water colour.

Viewed with awe
God's passion expressed in autumn leaves
rainbows after the mist
chipmunks foraging campsites
for bits of hot dog buns.

Felt comfortable in fellowship
fellow kindred souls conversing
round bonfire built for twenty
was glad just to be alive
living in the moment.

Viewed with awe
video games and hot tubs
T-shirts with logos and mountain pictures
branded on the chest
kids foraging parents for quarters
to play at the camp centre.

Unbathed for two days
smelled like a smokie without a bun
grey hair on a chin once hairless

SCOTT ALDERSON

Another Flush
viewed with awe
the value of friendship.

Damp Grass

Summertime
carly a.m.
two bodies gyrate
on moist grass

vocal chords stretch
moans into the silence that once was
but can be no more
this is the bed of passion
they chose to lie upon
this damp grass
that tickles her back

Summertime
later a.m.
two bodies rise
exchange farewells
and go off to work.

Old Mac

Old Macdonald had a farm
then the Government seized it
his cows, chickens, and pigs
his tractor, his till
e, i, e, i, o.

Old Mac declared bankruptcy
paid a lawyer big bucks
to tell his creditors
Old Mac was broke.

kept his home
kept his car
applied for a bank loan
to get back his animals
"Not for seven years."
the loans officer replied
"Not for a loser such as you."
the loan was denied.

"Welcome to welfare."
Old Mac we said
two minutes and a shotgun blast later
and Old Macdonald
was quite dead.

SCOTT ALDERSON

Feels Like You Died

Watching water from eyes
explode upon impact
with this blotted paper
feels like you died
in dream state I miss you
the tender times
far too rare
when the world didn't infect us
the quest for survival put on hold
for minutes, hours, days.

Where are you now?

Parrots

They sat as two parrots
sharing a branch
their beaks salivating
for the seeds of passion
filling their cage feeder.

They dined together
sharing the water trough afterwards
their large eyes meeting
for the need of recognition
validation of their bond.

They cawed as parrots
mated as lovers
wined and dined
shared some time
these animals
on display in the big pet store.

SCOTT ALDERSON

Pinhead

Security guard
asked me to vacate the seat
to which I'd developed a relationship
he said my tight ass
would tarnish the delicate marble
of which my throne was built.

as a martyr I rejected
his rude request
then sought to attack
his fragile $5.00 an hour psyche.

left him weeping as an infant.

Crack House

Property devalued in suburbia
when a brothel broke barriers
somehow got a license from the city
opened up right next door
coming and going all night
place full of pimps, place full of whores.

carelessly discarded condoms on grass
used I.V. needles litter the yard
somehow the neighbourhood is going down
where will the children play?
schoolyards swollen with gangs
is this the next wave?

vigilante groups forming in community
centres
cleanse chaotic cohabitants
chili dinner preachers sermon on Saturday
attend and convert
lost sheep in a house
with sheets used as drapes
so no light filters in.

Basement dwelling carpet scratchers
left suburbia
found a new heaven on the downtown
strip
watching buses and trains go by

SCOTT ALDERSON

Another Flush

sleeping under bushes,
every night, a camping trip.

Passion Remembered

Passions flame once lit my campfire
kept me warm while winter blanketed
ground around.

passion wore stay-up stockings
laid down upon my futon
and showed me how to love.

as a stereotype her red hair
keptthe fire burning
long enough to keep the warmth inside
before cold ashes remained
scattered in the pit.

years later on this new camping trip,
my fire won't ignite
no wood, no matches,
no flame burns this lonely night.

where are you passion?
do you still burn savagely?
is it healthy in your new home
or are you naked, empty, and all alone?
I remember you,
your touch, your scent
the inner beauty that made you glow
all the sweat that flowed

as a river headed toward the falls.   Another Flush

Peasant Anonymous

Responded to what had been read
in a newspaper classified,
attended announced meeting of
peasant anonymous
designed for those seeking recovery
from a disease of poverty

Living on street
diet lacking meat
scraps of glass and metal collected
to feed a daily addiction
working class without apartments
low vacancy and high rent
sleeping single file in a shelter
people camping in cars

Exited enlightenment to pretend
that a problem did not exist
then fell face first
into the deep end
joined a group
peasants anonymous
designed for those seeking recovery
from a disease of poverty

SCOTT ALDERSON

Fall Colours

Spectrum of fall colours
soon invade summer's landscape
seasons altered to induce hibernation.

Change
indeed
no more random attacks
on hikers and bikers
by berry addicted bears
no more random reports
of swimmers itch from man inspired lakes
no joggers, no rollerbladers
closure of outdoor pools
and a lawnmower seeks refuge
in a garden shed.

Change
indeed
where lies the mattress kitten
who seeks shelter
under my flannel bed sheets?

spectrum of fall colours
soon invade clothing fashions
seamlines altered to eliminate stimulation
bikinis and mothballs
stored in a cedar closet
bug spray taken to the landfill
another season of profit for the golf course

sees the opening of another ski hill
in a once protected provincial park.

Another Flush

Cold Debate

Does a farmer catch a cold
if he does not visit a city
during winter's reign?

Are airborne viruses and microorganisms
inside a country kitchen
floating in farmer's face?

Somewhere in an urban apartment
young child's cough echoes corridors
unconcerned as to origin of virus
that sought him as a host

were he on a farm
without a daycare to attend
would he now be sick?

down a street
an AIDS patient takes one last gasp of air
his blood transfusion years ago
when the tractor rolled on his leg
let the virus in.

In the end
a cold killed him
common to most
fatal to non-gay, non-drug-user

SCOTT ALDERSON

Another Flush

farmer types
who took blood transfusions in summer
some ten years ago.

Accurate Portrayal

I saw you and me
accurately portrayed
in a movie rented
from a major rental chain
within each frame of footage
they illustrated familiar pain
of a relationship cast aside
and in the end
a happy ending
not so for you and me

What happened to the entertain portion
of entertainment
tears lashing my weathered face
do not lead me to contentment
these pictures, these ghosts
these images of madness
make me feel ripped off
they charged money for this
taste of dysfunction

I saw you and me
in the faces of warriors
fresh from defeated battle
bandaged and bloodied
shell shocked and saddened
would they ever smile again?
I saw you and me
in the bottom of every alcoholic binge
in the last puff of a cigarette
in the last hoot from a joint

Why do I still wake up at night crying
years after we both died.

Another Flush

An accurate portrayal of divorce.

Leave a Message

I can't come to the phone right now
seem to be having a seizure
in the corner of my living room

not an epileptic
diabetic
having a stroke
just doing the funky chicken
might have been the toke
when someone pushed on my chest
while I inhaled,
this twitching
became the end result

I can't come to the phone right now
so leave a message
and if I don't slip into a coma
or end up brain damaged
or permanently institutionalized
I'll return your call.
THANK YOU.

SCOTT ALDERSON

Another Flush

Running Over People with My Bicycle

Clear sky sunny fall day
hyper mode on a busy street
traffic tight like a bag of potato chips
waiting to be opened and consumed,
within a maze of stalled cars,

suddenly,
pedestrian behind parked vehicle
not noticing black steel stallion
two wheeled spectre of impending collision
flesh and spokes connect
injury,
in the traffic court's decision
pedestrian was at fault
for showing poor judgement
bathed in his own excrement
several broken bones.

I remain unscathed
well-mannered and behaved;

I was running over people with my
bicycle years before
financial score
came from suing
we used to merely fight
day or night
warriors on the road well-travelled
decelerated from hyper mode
once the money was in my account.

SCOTT ALDERSON

Restaurant Misunderstanding

She spewed venom at the waiter
because her soup was cold
he didn't cook it,
but he sure got told
of its bland taste
diarrhea texture
virtual lack of pizzazz
and when he offered to return it
free of cost
she threatened to get him fired
demanded to speak to his boss
regarding his incompetence
he thought she said impotence
and knocked her on her ass

Unemployment suited him well.

All in Favour

Seems as though
sometimes we sacrifice
activities good for the soul
in favour
of those which
are good for the wallet

rarely does a choice exist
when a landlord shall insist
the payment is due
first of each month
for as long as tenancy
in a time of low vacancy
continues to enslave
every caveman
who needs a cave
for a family he can't afford.

Loss of artistic drive
spirit withers in favour of survive
cleaning washrooms
instead of writing poems
poetry pays not this peasant's rent
for his home

SCOTT ALDERSON

Another Flush   but a long drawn out verbal rant
time to pull up my pants
time to be
all in favour of living.

Complaint

I've heard enough of your voice
telling me how bad it is
that there is no choice,
pilot to co-pilot
we are going down in flames,
negative energy being exhausted
tearing down everything in sight
plumes of anger
shredding self-image
but this time
I don't react
instead find something to distract
to write off this bad day
to write off this bad attitude
tiring of conflict.

Devil on one shoulder, angel on the other
advocating different viewpoints
perspective altered just to stay alive
two sides of a coin
conversing with this host
but I've heard enough of your voice
telling me I'll never be happy
while the angel

says the reverse.　　　　　　　Another Flush

Danger

Many people seemed compelled
to warn him of the danger
choosing indeed to dwell
on the poverty stereotype
of a poet

no riches, no fame
only denial, literary shame
in a world dominated by
rock and roll heroes
false gods and trinkets
offered to them

many people acted jealous
as he turned his back to spite them
proving his poetic point
upon this planet
found his heaven.

　　　　SCOTT ALDERSON

Another Flush

Taste

Last night's taste
lingers in the next day,
the residue of your orgasmic juices
neither removed by soap nor water

a shower of memories
cannot wash away your scent,
and the ease to which you opened
astounded my experienced tongue

begging for bonding
flesh encompassing flesh
dance of ecstasy upon insertion
penetration pronounced pleasure.

Such Synchronicity

Such synchronicity should convince
any skeptic
two soulmates danced a ballet of love
two parrots shared a perch
two lovers entered desire
this past Sunday's eve

Longing lasting lavish periods of time
recreation of every sensual pleasure
within a mind
keeps passion fresh
keeps the hangover
from past Sunday's eve

When Wednesday
moves closer to Thursday
not a doubt remained
two lives indeed changed
from pure intensity
that came past Sunday's eve.

SCOTT ALDERSON

Detachment from the Umbilical Cord

Several days after his tenth birthday
a copy of an adult man's magazine
was discovered by his mother
· playing hide and seek
under his soft, brand-name mattress

did he know the soft texture
of the breast he admired
on sticky pages crusty touch?
was he already playing doctor roles
with the neighbourhood nurses?

so many thoughts troubling curious parent
who realizes their child
is a sexually curious being
questions come to mind
like how much does he know
who are the friends he has been seeing

Years to come following his tenth birthday
he developed an understanding

not from an adult man's magazine
but from experience
ongoing state of learning
how to moisturize
the canal he navigated
to find detachment
from the umbilical cord.

Fantasizing

Dilation of pupils
grin from dimple to dimple
a sudden "OH"
escapes chapped lips
busted
neon sign on forehead
reads
"WOW, YOU'RE AMAZING"
busted
visions of pleasure
flooding my mind
hips in motion
ready, set, grind
slowly, gently,
then picking up pace
like the rhythm of this poem
busted
written all over my face
no space to run
can't find a place
to release red from my cheeks
busted
"YES I WAS SCANNING YOU
APPRECIATING YOU

SCOTT ALDERSON

QUENCHING MY EYES
WITH HEDONISTIC DELIGHTS
ABSORBING YOUR ESSENCE"
busted
fantasizing.

Often

Caught on a couch
profound thoughts
medicated mental images
upon the daily deserts
where monotony is fought
by final retreat

isolation's curse
released when spring restores
colour to grass
cycling restores firmness
to my naked ass
animals mating

caught on a couch
often
while winter wrestles
with window frames
for dominance.

Salt and Pepper Shakers

Questions fly in suburban kitchens
like dishes smashed against a wall
parents debate loss of control
once generated over their child
now grown to adulthood

why do they carry carving instruments
and guns, into places of learning?

answers are lacking in suburban kitchens
is it choice of music
taste in clothes
or a diet of violent images
considered entertainment
movies, television
who knows?

this new generation
a salad of angry youths
searching salt and pepper shakers

SCOTT ALDERSON

Another Flush

of belonging
to identify with
shaken heavily
to bring out the flavour
pain observed
on cable television.

Importance

Importance is subjective
to one who is hungry
versus well fed
to one who is employed
versus home in bed
to pimp versus prostitute
wealthy to destitute
food bank provider \ donator
food bank consumer \ user
drug dealer
to drug abuser
mother \ father \ sibling
to child \ offspring

Importance is subjective
dependent on time of year
whether giving thanks
or Christmas cheer
New Year's \ birthday

any day to celebrate
in an area of peace
versus a time of war
in an arena of tolerance
versus wrestling ring of property claims
Middle East, Far East, Northeast, Southeast
importance is subjective
determined by where you exist.

Greetings

Greetings from the promise land
where rent control no longer exists
power surges follow friendly fee amendments
union disagreements persist
natural gas inflated by artificial increases
dictated by supply and subsequent
demand
forcing many to street shelters
addicted and alike
peasant sacrifice
working poor
so much more

which ancestor of Moses led us here?

SCOTT ALDERSON

Happy Valentine

Essence of our love
drips from team spirits
like a fire-teased marshmallow

world wakes with wonder
accurate portrayal of obsession/compulsion
Cupid's arrow piercing causes infection

essence of our love
allows for facing Goliath
permits pleasure found
outside dictionary columns

a natural miracle
in a time of natural disasters

Acknowledgements

The following deserve credit regarding
the development of this work:

Those who said it could not be done
those who said it could be
the believers and disbelievers
the critics and the muses
colleagues and associates
friends, family, lovers
my higher power.

The amateurs and veterans of life
teachers and healers
rebels and dealers
in the flush of life.

Special thanks to Peter Elzinga and Rein
Vanderkuil for their creative influences and
technical direction and bringing the dream
of Scott Alderson Poetry into a reality in
book form.

Think big, be big
Larger than life perhaps!

Keep writing.

Thanks,

Scott Alderson

The Happy Medium

Copyright 2005

Dedication

This work is dedicated to my ruby-emerald-sapphire-like being in a world of cubic zirconia's for Karen.

Introduction

Welcome to a fresh glimpse, a corner slice of mental pie. The Happy Medium was chosen for title after many hours of conversation and diversion. So often life situations fall into extremes.

Peace ------------------------------------- Crisis

I seek the happy medium; whether it is from the balance I maintain on the scales in my life, or trying to avoid a heart attack, a "stressed-out human" is neither productive, healthy, nor harmonious.

This past year has seen many births
and sad
faces
life of
new friends
death of
those whose
embrace I

279

once felt.

I hope
you enjoy this book
Be Well.

Feel the Wrath

Feel the wrath
poet's passionate fury
delivered by
bike courier's rush
sense the fear
listen
to the hush
words are weapons
be very afraid.

Actor

Life is like a movie
DVD wide-screen format perhaps
each year a single frame

You are the main character
with numerous supporting roles
a huge cast of extras
gorgeous leading ladies by the pool

Life is like a movie
playing in a theatre near you
no passes will be accepted
coupons will be rejected
so bring cold cash

SCOTT ALDERSON

Cruise With You

Resisted being a gold digger with nothing
Looking for a helpless victim with
something

Lived the street
Forced to not eat meat
Due to poverty not vegetarian option

A crisis rider
Happy soul tarnished by injustice
Taking from no one
Trudging a path of my own

So sell the BMW baby
Cause my Toyota has over 200,000
Kilometres
And my taste for caviar
Never developed thanks to a fish allergy

Resisted being a gold digger with nothing

Looking for a free ride towards something The Happy Medium
I merely want to cruise with you,
Changing driver's seat positions
At every rest stop pull-over area.

Mentor

I love you
floats too easily
in any air

I miss you
is far more powerful

Leonard Cohen taught me well
to observe
speculate
question
theorize
aspire
to bring
dreams to fruition
struggle
recover
rebuild
resurrect
reconnect
and he charged me minimal tuition
merely "The Energy of Slaves"

SCOTT ALDERSON

The Happy Medium

"Death of a Lady's Man"
and "The Spice Box of Earth"
collections of poetry
gospel enough to be mounted
on apartment bathroom walls

my mentor
I miss you
miles have been travelled
since I met you on the page
before Buddhist beckoning
prior to your own precious Rebecca
and my once precious affair

one day
I hope you miss me too.

Cohen Choir

I met Leonard Cohen
not in person
but, on page
when young adulthood held me

introduced by a woman
in person
not on page,
when she wanted to hold me

she met Leonard Cohen years prior

I delighted in his words,
in her company,
the three of us
filled a room with energy

I didn't know at the time
that he could sing
he doesn't know

SCOTT ALDERSON

that I can too.

Head Line

Friday morning newsprint read
"… as a result of tragic car accident, poet
dead."
tragic car accident
like there is any other kind.

Sharing Worms

Crows
Shared seeds Sunday in Sunnyside
I taunted them tactfully with high grade
grain
as the general population passed peacefully
in ignorant bliss
How about a kiss?

I see the poetry of life
feel passion of moments
observe universality in your once
lifeless eyes

Crows
counting individuals seems pointless
infinite and exhausting
approximate guess invite pain

SCOTT ALDERSON

The Happy Medium emotionless claws gripping branches of
civility
What is reality?

I have seen tree leaves bleed yellow from
green
felt saddened by season
found relief through love.

Leaves falling from trees
leaves, me introspective,
retrospective with fresh fragrance
tingling my essence

What has become
of the human condition
parents, daughters, sons
husbands, wives, same-sex situations?

Psychopaths on bike paths,
homeless hombres kicking addictions
Christian versus Muslim aftermaths
some symptoms of current afflictions

Diseases of the wind
diseases of the tree
shedding blood
shedding leaves

Look around in sadness as the seasons
change
feel a lump in the throat while reading
newsprint headlines
time is now to truly question all that is
underway
underfoot and slicing sideways into my
heart.

———

Happy Time

Generally I write about the rain not the sun
personal defeats instead of battles I have
won
so I thought I might try something different
not focusing on society or governments
choosing to feature memory re-runs
mental pictures of good songs sung

this poem took 38 years to write
happy times compounding, like a bank
account
so I could read it to you tonight

wish it were possible to recall
at one year old when father bathed me
and held my fragile body so I would not fall
smile in the photograph demonstrates

SCOTT ALDERSON

affection
not capturing father's condition
before cancer came to call

what I do remember is joy at age seven
five years after my dad went to heaven
when my sister Linda bought me a two
wheel bike
to replace the beaten tattered trike

this poem took 38 years to write
happy times selective, like songs on a
jukebox
yeah, heh, it's been a bizarre life

wish it were possible to describe
how I felt visiting Disneyland
my oldest sister taking me by the hand
first time away from Mom, almost terrified
advanced closer to becoming a man

what I can recollect is how it felt to marry
the love of my life, so extraordinary
so sweet, so luscious, so life-affirming
precious emotions, no more single-servings
this poem took 38 years to write
less than 5 minutes to read
and in the conclusion all I can say
is it had been an interesting life
chasing happy times
planting happy seeds
harvesting happy hay
turning my back on strife.

Labelling "You"

If a poem were written
for every uniqueness encountered
some would choose to point the pen
at themselves again
continuing the saga
an epic piece
about their time spent in my sphere

If they were offended
even though it was not intended
they might seek to harm
dislocate my arms
just to halt the mayhem
rationalizing that I wrote it for them
about them
dedicated
articulated

SCOTT ALDERSON

definitely
absolutely
without a doubt,
they are the "You"

hero or heroine
cocaine or heroin
victim or villain
persecuted or prosecutor
the significant others
demand recognition.

Untitled

Still uncertain
unsure whether my age is showing
or society is actually decomposing
littered with citizens lacking conscience,
like the middle-aged alcoholic picking up
empty bottles
with his brand new truck
out of alleyways where they were left for the
underprivileged
so they could live a better life,
or the funeral home that sold gorgeous
coffins
but burned the dead on sheets of cheap
plywood
still charging full price.

Untitled

Still sobbing
years after 800,000 Rwandan tribes people
were massacred
years after Baltic battles in Serbia and
Croatia
years after Vietnam, days into Iraq.

Has the era of the warrior come?

Peace is bullshit talk
festivals for hot dog vendors to sell their
product
peace is unattainable
when real estate costs so much.

Still rambling

SCOTT ALDERSON

The Happy Medium   jumping serious subjects
like unemployed on freight trains during
depression

Where is the hope?
Where is my dope?

Road Rage 3

Wish I had a jetpack
instead of a backpack
then I would chase that BMW
pull the driver to street level
hear bystanders shout
like fans at a hockey game
"get him, get him"

Wish I had a pill
instead of stubborn will
then I would wave at that BMW
chase the sunflower-sunfire driver
in the fast land
cycle past the slow
beamer-dreamer on his cell phone

Wish I had a loonie
instead of a nickel
for every good intention.

Ticket

At a busy intersection
traffic courting rush
perpendicular, vehicular
pedestrian, commotion
dancing dolphins in the urban pool

no bicycles allowed on concrete
don't disobey the signs
or, cops on concrete that you can't ride on
will issue lofty fines

compliance is complicated
defiance a choice
indifference, the cop-out
every pun intended

pinned against a car

SCOTT ALDERSON

The Happy Medium
busy intersection
traffic courting rush
when slowly from my bleeding lung
comes a final hush.

For Fudge

[This work is dedicated to Steve Gillespie
(A.K.A. – Eatlardfudge) Rest in peace old friend]

I want to believe, that people like you, when
they die,
become stars that guide nomads
for you were so brilliant and shining
gifted with wisdom and words
to let others see
the spirit within
now serving to direct weary travellers.

I want to believe that you are reacquainting
yourself
with your Mother and others
that left this life before you,
my selfish nature wishes you could have
remained

for one more chance to express   The Happy Medium
how much
I cherished our friendship and camaraderie

So many peace pipes smoked between us
poets
so many faces have said goodbye
over years the casualties are mounting
another great artist gone

No one else made me laugh as hard as you
in the literary salon at Annie's Books
Company in Calgary

Tuesday night poetry reading
When you were Steve Gillespie
poet from Victoria,
who grew up in a dysfunctional home
had a dysfunctional heart
never fully recovered mentally or physically
became dysfunctional
who I called friend

I want to believe that people like you,
when they die,
leave behind people
like me,
to tell others how genuine you were.

SCOTT ALDERSON

Broken Frame

[This work is dedicated to Steve Gillespie
(Eatlardfudge)]

I remember the road trips to Edmonton
the tour through the government buildings
smoking a joint with you under security
camera
Karaoke madness and cheap motel rooms

I recall your blood sugar being low
lack of insulin and syringe
lack of preparedness
lack of caring

Unlike the world,
you were kind
animal lover
Environmentalist

eco-friendly, just pure friendly
except those black days
spent cultivating withdrawal
when demons from the past prodded
and poked viciously from all sides
until your covered face with hands and cried
like an infant
needing parental comforting

I held you many times
man to man
friend to friend
I supported your frame.

Totem Pole

Her aboriginal name
when translated to English
was "she who complains too much"
I called her "dear"

For months they listened
sweat lodged and pow wowed
over how men had mistreated her
leaving four husbands howling
like wolves trapped then shot
tranquilizer needles to reach tranquility
till the divorce papers were served
hot and tender

Aboriginal people remember her spirit
I find it easier to recall her anger

SCOTT ALDERSON

as it was frequently focused on me.

Word Seizure

Acting so nervous around me
nearly shaking,
twitching,
whole body itching
to get away from my
words,
scaring
freaking you out,
words
not tender, not harnessed
ripping your psyche
words
directed with harmful precision
nonphysical incision
words
directed at you.

SCOTT ALDERSON   *300*

Disoriented

Awkward adolescent in secondary school
caught my attention when he blocked my
path
to tell me "I was cool"
in his limited opinion
influenced by parents, peers, and media hype
lord of his dominion
said I struck him as the nonconformist type

lost my focus when to my leg landed a
locust
and the teen became obscene
began discussing globalization
politics and pesticide elimination
I left disoriented.

SCOTT ALDERSON

Bite

Dropped out of routine
to challenge comfort zones
cancelled cable television subscriptions
reduced amounts of daily prescriptions
without any doctor advice

bit by mosquito
with West Nile bile
infected with the virus

tried hard not to get excited
latest threat from bloodsuckers
got me scared not delighted
afraid to go outside shelter
lacking channels and drugs

every day brings challenge

walking across an urban street
could result in fatality
mosquito bite in backyard
can alter physical abilities
leaving me labelled
bitten.

Loose Gerbil

Fourteen years ago
acting as a King
I dubbed him "Gerbil"
as familiar as panhandlers
to those whose
office is the outdoors

His wire-rimmed outdated eyeglasses
erratic curly hair
eccentric behaviour
and unmedicated rage
make him a sociological study case

The only solace he seeks
is a coin return slot in a newspaper box
the only distraction
is a police reaction when he walks into
traffic

SCOTT ALDERSON

usually going the wrong way

He is an icon
a rare bird
a deviant for sure
one day I hope to shake his hand
before he shakes me off my bike.

Breakfast

I dream about you more   of late
together having breakfast
sharing corn flakes

Big bouncing bundles of water
encased in flesh,
woke up exhausted
in a Saturday mess

Dreams become reality   of late
no more am I alone
forced to contemplate

Pretty petite pigments adorn you
freckles on your chest
attending to each one of them
puts my tongue to test.

Fed

FED on a diet of insults
delivered by a man
with a fabric noose around his neck
shoes made from animal hides
found it quite uncomfortable
for he smile as he fully denied
his attire could feed a family of four

Laughing maniacally
attacking status ego's
class distinction
class disgust
class dismissed
lesson of life learned
spoken word is lethal

Shaking hands, deal complete

SCOTT ALDERSON

The Happy Medium   one in victor, one in defeat
exchange cards
wave bye bye
one left to laugh
one left to cry.

Crisis in Iran

Urban apartment Friday night in January
sub-arctic temperatures create the silence
rubber tires on slippery surfaces,
while an Earthquake slices suburbia
in the land of Ayatollah whoever

1-800-FED EX ships relief packages
to a populace that prefer the evil Christian
dead
than take gratitude in the form of a blanket
or a tent to shelter their heads
from Islamic rain and thunder

Hurls me outside prairie winter
pondering problems with nonobvious
solutions

SCOTT ALDERSON

blood is blood
blood is red
is this black and white thinking?
then so be it.

Death in the Family

Visited the widow on Christmas Day
she thanked me for taking time to talk
said that other people were avoiding her
at least so she thought

I was taken with near shock
time ticking as we talked
six months to a year from now
she would reunite with her dear husband
of four decades treasured

In death did they part
wounded widow wears broken heart
sobs ceremoniously and with conviction
proclaims to an empty silence
that she is not an apparition
asks for acknowledgement

307

SCOTT ALDERSON

when the room is full

I cried with her during Christmas
celebrations
shared my memory of a groom gone
she reminded me of my sensitivity
where had it disappeared to for so long?

Rambling Once Again

In residence
inner city apartment
miniscule square footage
no storage compartment

refrigerator hums like a retired gentleman
oven thaws window frost during winters'
wrath

I am alone on Saturday night
been here many times before
screeching out my boredom
neighbours knocking at my door

toilet flushes without human assistance
bed with worn springs nearly touches floor

I am contemplating existence   The Happy Medium
that place just short of a life
recognizing monotony in the mirror.

Dean

Dean died December 15, 2003
left memories of 13 years cycling courier
madness
fresh inside me

I did not know him from coffee house chats
nor pointed my nose into his life
instead called him friend and fellow warrior
combating icy winter winds

two months ago we shared a peace pipe
in a back urban alleyway
with homeless stereotypes and business suits
observing
from loading dock perches

I will be at Dean's funeral
I will smoke the pipe in the alleyway

SCOTT ALDERSON

in tribute a year from now.

A Tango is a One-Night Stand

Saturday evening in an urban game farm
many creatures rise from their dens
seeking alcohol nourishment at a singles bar
young chicks, old hens
pop-star-look-a-like boys
and old men
packaged tightly
sharing squares on a dance floor

how many relationships take form tonight?
will they continue into morning light?
or,
will the break of dawn
shine truth upon
loneliness?

"I'll call you sometime," he said
"That would be nice," she responded
exchanging wrong phone numbers
fake smiles and false e-mail addresses

Scott Alderson

while awkward smiles appear on foreheads The Happy Medium
    a close body embrace
    fleeting glances
as he exited her apartment lobby door.

    how many lovers danced last night?
    was a waltz on the dance card
    or a tango in clear sight?

Sunday morning in an urban game farm
    a creature returns to his den
nursing hangovers from the singles bar
trying to recall neon memories of where he
        had been
        things he had seen
        people he had met
    the bed in which he slept

answers came in the form of a business card
    spider slipped into his silk suit blazer
it read: Get to a clinic for an AIDS test for I
        am HIV positive.
    Signed, Tango lover.

SCOTT ALDERSON

Camaraderie

Find yourself being labelled
different, unique, unusual, perhaps deviant?

Are you isolated, prone to jotting thoughts
onto any transferable item available?

Do you contemplate constantly
pondering political noncompliance?

Chances are, you may be a writer.

Novel, short story, drama, romance,
mystery, or poetry
a collage of rejection letters in publisher
files
could be the place you seem to be

Camaraderie calls from this voice of mine

Before belief in dreams is lost

before loss of hope assaults another spiritThe Happy Medium
before the pen is put down
abandoned

I beg you

Seek

Form congregations
solid foundations
with writers in your community
together forge solidarity
to announce the word

camaraderie in my exquisite present
removing me from past
propelling uncertain futures

Is necessary
for me to keep faith
to face the audience
to thank mentors and peers.

SCOTT ALDERSON

Another Day in October

Fortune cookie message from soup kitchen
was difficult to decipher
for it lacked freshness
contained no mercy
basically read like a eulogy

"A kind person needs no wealth, only spirit
to thrive"

subsequently,
doing dishes developed into a philosophy
session
even the alcoholic had something to say
about wisdom from a company writer
whose wealth came from cookies
who never ate from a soup kitchen.

Love You More Than...

LOVE you more than macaroni and cheese
Single serving size from the shelter
More than the dog coated with fleas
That wants me to pet him in bad weather
Soaked with water
Macaroni soaked with too much milk

LOVE you more than nicotine
From packages with nasty photos on the
cover
More than black stockings on toned legs
That call to me as a lover
Indulgence tempting
Enjoyment pending

LOVE you more than hot bath for aching
muscles
Bubble surface madness in a tub
More than oatmeal on a cold morning
Warms me all cuddly like a black bear cub

315   SCOTT ALDERSON

Soothing heat
Illusion entered.

Live Show

Observed and appreciated poetry presented
on every occasion that permitted
tear-drenched denims from humour
or tear-stained sweater shoulders
from uncommon valour

Felt tickles the first time I made an audience
wet with my words,
rejoiced, when my political satire
made the man in the suit perspire,
glowed when someone said
"I completely related to what you were
saying"

Sat in library basements on Friday evenings
tasting poetry laced with family, surgery, and
resolve
while audience required permission for
applause
enjoyed the difference between live

versus reading off the page.   The Happy Medium

Sacrificed social life for social problems
no looking in rear view mirror
spent decades as a poet
all my existence so far.

Loving each blessed moment
except the visit to welfare
the ultimate live show.

Playing with Mines

"How rude" thought the minimum-wage-
grunt
behind the plastic counter,
when she asked if there was anything else
she could get me today
and I responded
that same way when eight years old and an
artificial Santa
asked me the identical question,
I said, "How about world peace?"
her face drew and expression
as if she had just stepped on a landmine.

How futile felt the peaceful warrior when
followed
by an alcoholic breath, no fixed-address
individual
for half a city sidewalk stretch
realizing he was powerless to rid this mess
from clogging city sewer systems
decided to simply ignore the intrusion

SCOTT ALDERSON

The Happy Medium until the mutant of sub-human conditions
found a more suitable donor for a cash
advance.

How hostile reacted the military commander
when one of his soldiers stepped on a mine,
or was it a "yours"?

Who knows.
How agile the politician became, bent over a
corporate desk in a president's office
how compliant, how complacent, how
completely capable of handing over natural
resources and revenues
to a prince of darkness.

"Hell is living" said the outpatient as he
passed in the hall.

Is it a mine, or is it a yours?

How negative his whole being became over
he past few months' whispers
through an Internet e-mail network,
how arrogant and almost antagonistic for
certain
shedding decency in favour of survival,
sold his ass on the street in negative
temperatures
to negative dicks, negative chicks
negative battery terminals
in a totally grounded world.

Academia

The academics have taken over Edmonton
Stroll of Poets that is
more lethal than an unpronounced word
these prophets of poetry
define boredom bravely

Street level is different
no critique when in crisis
what kind of bureaucrat do they think they
are?

Go back to school graduate fool
leave diction tucked in your pants
I was exposed on paper
long before it was on the back of the film
your father took of your mother.

SCOTT ALDERSON

Dino Dreads September

Cold puppies cry incessantly
frosty Sunday October front yards
whining for Wilma to hit the remote
heated-double-garage-heaven

With Fred fixing flats
Barney bingeing beers
Betty baking bread
Bam-Bam bearing biceps
Dino dampens dreams of warmth

Pebbles in an alleyway
frosty Sunday October backyards
leaves left for Mr. Slate to rake
Flintstone fever in a quarry.

Bass Fever

Awoke to past memories
seeping through my damned brain
slivers causing pain

Viewed bass guitar from afar
grabbed a pick to tickle it
with lovers tender fingertips
calloused knuckles cut on frets
how much better can it get?

Punished subversive neighbours
Sunday morning 7:01 a.m.

Bass fever swelling
hatching horrific headspace
last night party central down the hall
elicited a response dignified,
consider the message sent.

SCOTT ALDERSON

Bass Bacon Bits

Bass guitar begs attention
neglected for days, weeks
too many other distractions
in hours, minutes, months
finger broken unable to tweak
four strings feverishly

worry about debt left to fret
chords of bankruptcy
polluting environment where magic sits in a
stand
crying, screaming "play me, play me."

Bass guitar begs attention
continuous
amplifier plugs itself into wall outlet
electric hum
distinguishable

No time for play
to play
be play.

They Come From Good Homes

While crackheads are crashing cop cruisers
spike belts laid out but ineffective
crack commando teams are kicking cannabis
growers
leaving broken doorframes
broken homes
across sidewalks from schools
teenage hoodlums wearing "dew rags"
from broken homes
broken doorframes
abusive stepfathers
addict sons
prostitute daughters
crack commando cracking down on
Canadian growers
leaving broken doorframes
broken homes.

323   SCOTT ALDERSON

No Title

Don't know if I'm dictatorial
but I'm definitely territorial
so don't touch what's righteously
Mine.

I Write My Rhyme

Sometimes
when a wound is not so fresh
trust put to the test
betrayal
untarnished by coated tongue.

I write
disappointment
choices clearly communicated
bad decisions manifest
another friendship bites
the big pepperoni stick.

SCOTT ALDERSON

Winter Screams

Winter screams
as a zebra colt
forced to the ground
by a pride of lions

The colt fights
legs thrash violently
till lions' teeth
eliminate life

Lions live another day
scavengers pick the colt
somewhere over salty oceans
winter screams
at Man's arrogance.

2 Businessmen

Someone dropped a cellular phone
into a garbage bin
still functioned more than adequately
wonder what came over him.

Someone else threw a pager
out a 45th floor window
still functioned more than adequately
so the man decided to follow.

Hit the pavement simultaneously
as the cell phone hit the trash
2 businessmen cracking adequately
still functioning but no cash.

SCOTT ALDERSON

Prime Minister

Prime Minister pushed a pinhead
who got fiercely in his way
beat an assault rap
cause it was a protest
staged on flag day.

Apology accepted sinister minister
just don't get in my way
for if you react like a human
then for me it is also okay.

You made the news that day
Mr. Minister I must say,
Surely you could have found
a better way.

Never and Always

Never wanted to be
captured in the public eye,
these words
precious somewhat simple
are for your eyes only.

Never required the view of many
seemed more content in anonymity,
these days
rooms are crowded
we're on display.

Always stopped to stroke a flower
seems I'm too busy too distracted
these evenings
I watch the Sun set alone.

SCOTT ALDERSON

Most

Most of my lovers
have abandoned me
sometime, someway
seems to me a shame
state of this magnificent planet
state of shambles these days

Most of my admirers
have admired me
sometime, someway
made their stand against society
in hopes that it would change;
more human than we're been
people before anything else
reaching out for understanding
more than just ourselves.

Most of my fantasies
have been bestowed upon me
submissive and dominant
seems to me a shame

state of this magnificent planet
state of shambles these days

Most of my lovers learned something from
me
sometime, someway
seemed to me a symbiotic relationship
state of unique bonding
state of existence in an alternate
cave.

Arctic Wind

Through the arctic wind
amidst falling ice crystals
a warm spirit sings
a promise of tomorrow.

An uplifting of being
fresh frost on her lips
soothing voice,
gives permission to dream.

Through the morning darkness
amidst awakening emotions
fair maiden resounds a greeting,
"Do you take sugar and cream?"

    SCOTT ALDERSON

Hand

Plane unless tanned
skin on bone
knuckles lacking brass
this I dub
my lowly hand

Did you kill brother Abel?
fleshly beast at the end of my
arm
Did you seek revenge
upon those who worked
calluses
on the surface?

Lines of life
run in rhythm
towards ceramic nails
gracing your top
oh sacred hand.

Parasite

Some parasitic organism
is sucking blood out of society
an unidentified creature
whose bite destroys families.

Divorce rate 50 percent
social chaos rampant
are we doomed?
are we damned?

Lawyers love the parasite
in secret chambers they worship
while their helium wallets
float in their back pockets.

Dysfunctional families on the rise
statistics increasing with every new day
children acting out in schools
the pain they feel today.

New music angry
unparalleled violence
from today's new voice

SCOTT ALDERSON

reflecting the bad news
of a world created
a world with limited choice.

The parasite grows hungry
as the host is nearly drained
who will be brave enough
to lynch the leech
to bring us out of pain?

We seek a Messiah
a scapegoat from the swamp
to restore family balance
to defeat the parasitic bump.

Careful not to crucify
the separator from the host
the repairer of the damage done
the saviour out of my reach.

Day Off Without Pay

Bid farewell to another tyrant growing in a
wage-earner environment
more lack of considerations for individuality
case of corporate greed
business needs
was it so difficult
to appreciate my talents?

Future forecast calls for severe storms

Bid farewell to another moment
another precious breath
expelling control-obsessed supervisor
from a warehouse war

Another minute just passed on a tropical
island

I missed it.

SCOTT ALDERSON

Moment 39

Spent a whole day in withdrawal from you
sugar sweet sentiments,
so clear now in the hunger
so pristine is the moment
so resounding the crash
reality is not a drug
to be smoked occasionally.

Adjustment

Non-resident manager
dressed
identified
by fabric tied
tightly round his neck
speaking authority-like
in letterbox memorandum
addressed
to yours truly
sincerely, respectfully
and so on

proclaiming increases
monthly rent inflating
without helium assistance
making apartments unaffordable
unlike those major department store
commercials,
there is no price slashing going on here
only peasant jugulars

SCOTT ALDERSON

I won't need a VCR
dishwasher, fireplace, washer, dryer
microwave nor refrigerator
when at street level

No university degree nor government panel
required
to comprehend homelessness
seem to be understanding it quite well

Fugitive

Late model man
with outrageous kilometres
on an alcohol-based engine
took issue with yours truly recently
looked at me through cracked windshield
opened oral window

"You sir, are a fugitive"
slight pause to collect intellect
"from the barber shop"
he continued with saliva building,
cowboy hat tilted to his right

Earlier model poet
with outrageous hairstyle
on a caffeine-based engine
decided not to take issue with greeting
responded with ambiguity

"Whatever."

Killing Bugs on a Saturday Morning in a One-Bedroom Basement Suite

Glass panes move aside
allowing urban air to circulate
exhaust fumes and voices not familiar
into a familiar dwelling

invasions from outdoors
move indoors
take physical form
crawl on cheap carpet

get slammed!!
by yesterday's newsprint

ink on cover
blotches red

SCOTT ALDERSON

human drone enjoys glory
breakfast cereal
music at extreme volume
punk rock stories

Leader Has a Problem

Considering that the government used to
deal alcohol
why would it surprise a commoner like me
to learn the leader has an issue,
a decreased sense of tolerance
an addiction by any other name
a dis ease about him?

Several years ago I would be drinking
alongside him
in a small town tavern or a homeless shelter
talking politics to the point of intoxication
interrupted by smashing jug of draft brew
over conservative and liberal attitudes,
my social credits redeemed
today's democracy askew
leaning toward extreme
bordering totalitarian.

Cheers!!!

Twinkle

Speak not of love to me today
it seems as foreign as computer operations

instead,
tell me I am a twinkle
a night blemish
belonging to the Universe

on bad days
name a tornado after me

do not label love

love appears more demanding
rigid
sacrificial, prejudicial
biased in a belief in forever
dust to soil
parted in the end.

Ran out of hope before paper.

SCOTT ALDERSON

Sexual Partners

One to show you how
One to break your heart
One to enjoy happily ever after.

Greeting Card 17

Been blessed by buddies
for quite awhile
friends that bend as I
to greet life's challenges
some make us smile
some make us cry.

Road Test

New vehicle
new to me
performed exceptionally
outran blizzard
on my tail
like coyotes to a rabbit
reformed field of concrete
brought me safely home to you.

Realized recently
world is lonely
world is empty
world is void
without you.

Road test resulted in purchase
extended warranties
extra protection
lifetime roadside assistance
with you.

Banned Breed

Reputation of insanity
lockjaw amputee bite
guard dog beware
mighty pit bull enters arena

Staffordshire father
mastiff grand
bred purely to annihilate
Shih Tzu opponents

Junk yard dogs don't
blend well as family pets

Mean people mean dogs
spiked leather collars
choke chain conversations
with man's best friend
kicked, punched, beaten
what kind of dog food is he eating?
forcing him to puke.

SCOTT ALDERSON

Finished

Fed up
with false promises of ending poverty

World economy
first world, third world
has to exist
for first to boom
I get it!

I don't accept it.

Fed up
finished.

Neighbours
won't accept shelters in suburbia
real estate value depreciates
with every soup kitchen line up.
So shut up!
quit shouting through the media
that some things are going to change
it's all cheap talk.

I am so finished.

Acknowledgements

Karen for typesetting and data entry.

Mom, Kevin, Sandra, Sharon, Linda, Troy,
Shauna, Brian,
Angela, Amanda, Tony, Jalryna, Neil, Dana
Alicia, April, Meaghan, Savannah, and
Taylor

John and Melissa (Front cover graphic
design)
Lyndsay
Uncle Casey
Steve (R.I.P.)

Cam, Kellie, Rich, Judy
Gord MacLennon
Fenna
Gary Buxton
Boardwalk Writers of Calgary
Society of Poets, Bards,& Storytellers
Hawkeye Studios
Ken Davies

The Facebook Collection

November 12, 2014 to April 15, 2017

These were poems written on Facebook and now published in this anthology for the first time.

April 15, 2017

Things are Getting Tense

While winter's wrath blankets Edmonton area with precipitation
we who watch from the South
view with open mouth
a World on the verge
of annihilation

China calling casually
some young guy
asking for hostilities
to be cast aside
North Korean chaos
talking to you Mr. You
does he see me
through the camera in my microwave?

Miles away
just another day
in Trump's tumultuous tyranny

Some young guy
pleading for calm

349

SCOTT ALDERSON

to carry on
no Saturday morning cartoon

May you all be safe
in the April blizzard
all-weather weirdness
all-world madness

April 2, 2017

Welcome to another addition of April, National Poetry Month. My
latest, composed while sitting here, now.

There are times of no poetry
when all that is clear
around here
is such silent sadness
unspoken madness
in a crispy spring downpour

Tomorrow when waking
awareness of
what would have been
my Mother's birthday

Tonight while viewing
awards of music
what could have been
a tribute to Leonard Cohen

Delivered in English and French
no mention of his poetic greatness
prime politician pondering
well water whisked in my eyes

There are times of no poetry
but the battle continues
I am greeted by gratitude
and appreciate your indulgence.

December 27, 2016

Game Show 2016

Time to play
which celebrity dies today
every twenty-four hours
leaves my tongue sour

We lost Prince
now the Princess Leia
no more "Postcards from the Edge"
no more doves crying

What happened to George Michael?
Was it a drug cycle he pedaled to demise?
Enjoyed his music, gave us "Faith"
"Father Figure" and "One More Try"

Spin the wheel
pick a letter
"Watership Down"
Author passed away

Each day heralds
a new announcement

SCOTT ALDERSON

Live each as if it were the last
cannot change the past
carry on wayward sons and daughters,
peace be with you all.

September 23, 2016

Three weeks earlier
in prayer, I let you go
compassionate and caring
memories searing
gave governing God permission
to guide you from pain

Selfishly lonely
passing your room daily
ghosts speak with your voice
memories searing
who will chase the monsters away now?

June 25, 2016

Mom screams like a tortured POW
when they come to change her diaper
unaware, unsure, unsecure
strangers touching her
threats all around

I have prayed for miracles
God has his answering machine on
I left multiple messages

Mom does not eat
asks the same questions,
complains that she does not feel good
despite the drugs
nurses administer

Sounds one should not hear
escape Mom's hospital room
I scream silently like a tortured POW

SCOTT ALDERSON

June 10, 2016

I did not grow up watching hockey with my Father
Dad passed away when I was 22 months of age,
but I know who Wayne Gretzky is
how could I not know Gordie
Mr. Hockey
Mr. Coffee of the ice
I use 2 wheels to propel
he used 2 skates, how nice;
how sad to see the passing
one legend after another
shows I am aging.

June 4, 2016

Cassius Clay went away yesterday
Ali answered another challenge
in the boxing ring he danced so well in
the solid striking left
and a righteous right
he punched in heaven's door
tired of knocking

Floating like the butterfly
stinging like the bee
I watched you religiously

Rest in peace.

May 19, 2016

Still affected by their anguish
still seriously sobbing
years after their children died
victims of a mad man's blade

Still affected by the everyday
still smiling seriously
though the crevices caress cheeks
from keeping it all inside

Even the Prime Minister
turns sinister
when the crap carries on

We are but human after all
crushed like ice for a cocktail
standing tall before a fall.

Hope your day is not gray
remembering the Brentwood 5
young adults slain in May.

January 17, 2016

Jack was back in his Cadillac
not a "smart" car,
to go with his smart phone and "energy star" appliances
just another 1970's big boat
in a big world with big people
with a big tank and low gas prices.

Jack sat steadfast in his Cadillac
feasting on a Wendy's "Baconator"
and like Arnold the Terminator,
he knew he'd be back.

What is the point
he thought as he lit his third joint
and drove his boat into the Lake
man-made or natural
it sunk that car in minutes.

Jack was back to walking to Wendy's.

SCOTT ALDERSON

January 11, 2016

For a Legend, David

My heroes are dying
some strange space oddity
shell shocked saddened by the news
that in the church of rock and roll legends pews
an empty chair remains

He told us to dance
catch the paper boy
go to Suffragette City
turn to the left, fashion
this Rebel, rebel hot tramp
told me about a Star man
thought he'd blow my mind

Bye bye Bowie
young and old Canadians salute you
I too am afraid of Americans, sometimes
Ashes to Ashes
I knew Major Tom was a junkie
and in my Golden years under pressure,
I feel the Changes,
Rest in Peace.

December 16, 2015

9 days before Christmas and all through Facebook
were postings about politics, recipes for food to cook

Bored with such, went to the mall
watched consumer credit card chaos
subsequent credit ratings fall

Got in line to see Santa
children viewed me with awe
elves and candy cane girls
could not believe what they saw
I navigated power chair
through Santa's North Pole lair
but could not transfer onto his lap
woke the overweight man from his nap

He asked me what I wanted for Christmas
I told him the cure for Multiple Sclerosis
left him disoriented.

SCOTT ALDERSON

December 3, 2015

First Draft

What Stimulus provoked the Killing Spree?

Did you wake up this morning out of sorts?
Cast aside the medication that helped you feel normal
grabbed the gun you bought last sale at K-Mart
and vented on innocent people

Why didn't you phone someone?
A friend, the distress centre, anyone

Struggling to understand
what went wrong
in the Utopian plan

The focus has been
on those unseen
the terrorist from overseas

What evil unleashed deep inside you?
Wish we could have talked it out
then we would not be left wondering
cause and subsequent event

on every news channel shouting it

Whatever disturbed you
May you now find rest.

November 10, 2015

In dream state I soar with Angels
fight Demons and demonstrate kindness
to those who remain interested

I intersect intersections on my bicycle
unaware of any disability

In dream state I fantasize
envision world without war
visit your bedside

I travel through dimensions to save everyone
hoping that someone, anyone
feels the world worthy of redemption

In dream state I am successful
in bridging the gap
between happiness and despair

I awaken close to a wheelchair
initials engraved, same as mine.

SCOTT ALDERSON

September 16, 2015

Tear ducts leaking at ten a.m.
Two year old victim remains located
I never claimed to understand divine will
left asking questions about why and how
tears continue still
I hope God held you as you passed.

February 27, 2015

"Spock to Enterprise, one to beam up"
God listened to the communicator
welcoming the actor Leonard Nimoy
into his Mother Ship.
Rest in peace, you lived long
and made my spirit prosper.
Never expected to weep from Star Trek
but "Wrath of Khan" tore my heart apart
When Spock says to Captain James T. Kirk
"I have and always will be your friend,"
I personalized it and thought of my own friends.
And when Kirk speaks at the funeral and says, "Of all the souls I have
met in
the Universe, his was the most, human."
I cried, I still cry thinking about it, no macho crap here.
Entertainment Tonight misses you Leonard Nimoy
I do too.

SCOTT ALDERSON

January 13, 2015

Something New to Suckle

Corporate coyotes caressing laminate dance flooring
Christmas chaotic celebrations with alcohol-induced jubilations
banquet buffet breakfast, bacon-stuffed stomachs put to test

I observed from wheelchair
sobbing at the loss of self
former person dancing in dreams.

Kardashian clones cleansing pores
sweating sweetly under unrehearsed speeches
and alcoholic Karaoke crooners, entertained us under Mountain moon

enjoyed a moment, appreciated madness
avoided hot tub, surrendered to sadness
only for a second or two

I observed from wheelchair
Noticed a costume change
tortured heavy metal lyrics
put to dance boom box beats
corporate coyotes gone insane,
entertained us under Mountain moon.

November 12, 2014

Scott's first post on Facebook:

Started Working at Retired

SCOTT ALDERSON

Made in the USA
San Bernardino, CA
21 August 2017